STOKING THE CREATIVE FIRES

Stepping Stones, Kyoto Rock Garden.
Photograph by Phil Cousineau, 1986.

BOOKS BY PHIL COUSINEAU

The Hero's Journey: Joseph Campbell on His Life and Work 1990

Deadlines: A Rhapsody on a Theme of Famous Last Words 1991

The Soul of the World: A Modern Book of Hours (with Eric Lawton) 1993

Riders on the Storm: My Life with Jim Morrison and the Doors (John Densmore with Phil Cousineau) 1993

Soul: An Archaeology: Readings from Socrates to Ray Charles 1994

Prayers at 3 A.M.: Poems, Songs, Chants for the Middle of the Night 1995

UFOs: A Mythic Manual for the Millennium 1995

Design Outlaws: On the Frontier of the 21st Century (with Chris Zelov) 1996

Soul Moments: Marvelous Stories of Synchronicity 1997

The Art of Pilgrimage: The Seeker's Guide to Making Travel Sacred 1998

Riddle Me This: A World Treasury of Folk and Literary Puzzles 1999

The Soul Aflame: A Modern Book of Hours (with Eric Lawton) 2000

The Book of Roads: Travel Stories 2000

Once and Future Myths: The Power of Ancient Stories in Modern Times 2001

The Way Things Are: Conversations with Huston Smith on the Spiritual Life 2002

The Olympic Odyssey: Rekindling the Spirit of the Great Games 2003

The Blue Museum: Poems 2004

Angkor Wat: The Marvelous Enigma (Photographs) 2005

A Seat at the Table: Struggling for American Indian Religious Freedom 2005

The Jaguar People: An Amazon Chronicle (Photographs) 2006

Night Train: New Poems 2007

The Meaning of Tea (with Scott Hoyt) 2008

Stoking the
Creative Fires

9 WAYS TO REKINDLE
PASSION AND IMAGINATION

Phil Cousineau

Conari Press

First published in 2008 by Conari Press,
an imprint of Red Wheel/Weiser, LLC
With offices at:
500 Third Street, Suite 230
San Francisco, CA 94107
www.redwheelweiser.com

Art permissions can be found on p. 222

ISBN: 978-1-57324-299-8
Library of Congress Cataloging-in-Publication Data

Cousineau, Phil.
Stoking the creative fires : 9 ways to rekindle passion and
imagination / Phil Cousineau.
        p. cm.
Includes bibliographical references.
ISBN 978-1-57324-299-8 (alk. paper)
1. Creative ability. 2. Imagination. I. Title.
BF408.C674 2008
153.3—dc22
                    2007049625

Cover and text design by Brooke Johnson
Typeset in Sabon and Scala Sans
Cover art: *Fire Dream,* oil on linen, copyright © 2002
by Gregg Chadwick

Printed in Canada
TCP
10 9 8 7 6 5 4 3 2 1

CONTENTS

*This book is dedicated
to the memory of
Gary Rhine,
whose creative fire
lives on in his films,
his family,
and his friends.*

Acknowledgments

I want to express my gratitude to those who have read or discussed the ideas in this manuscript or provided inspiration during my research, including Gregg Chadwick, R. B. Morris, Karly Stribling, Gerry Nicosia, Fr. Gary Young, Joanne Warfield, Stuart Balcomb, Ty Gram, Robin Eschner, John O'Brien, Antler, Jeff Poniewaz, Laila Carlson, Keith Thompson, David Darling, Michael Guillen, John Nance, John Borton, P. J. Curtis, Gary Bolles, Anthony Lawlor, Fr. John Dear, Toni D'Anca, Jean Erdman, Alexander and Jane Eliot, and my friends at Eguna Basque café in North Beach, San Francisco, and Elise Jajuga, whose father Mike Jajuga would have been very proud of her work in publishing. Thanks, too, to my colleagues at Red Wheel, especially Brenda Knight and Jan Johnson, whose faith in my creative fire made this book possible; creative director Donna Linden whose guidance made it graceful; designer Brooke Johnson and the rest of the Red Wheel/Weiser/Conari team, including Rachel Leach, Jordan Overby, Caroline Pincus and Jan Hughes who all made the journey enjoyable. I also wish to express my thanks to my agent Amy Rennert for her enthusiastic, stalwart help with this project. Most of all, loving thanks to Jo Beaton and Jack Cousineau for teaching me how to create a life together.

A Fable about Fire

by Leonardo da Vinci (from Prophecies)

The stone, feeling itself struck by flint, was astonished and said in a stern voice, "How can you be so presumptuous as to trouble me? Stop upsetting me. You have given me a blow as though in revenge, and yet I have never annoyed anyone."

To this the flint replied, "If you will be patient, you will see a marvelous result." The stone calmed down and bore its sufferings with patience and fortitude, and saw itself give birth to a marvelous fire that was so powerful that it was useful for many things.

This is relevant to those who are fearful as they begin their studies, and then when they become able to control themselves and continue patiently with their studies, find that they achieve things that are marvelous to see.

Irish Knot of Eternity Tombstone. County Clare, Ireland, 1980.
Photograph by Phil Cousineau.

The Creative Journey

O for a Muse of fire that would ascend
The brightest heaven of invention.

William Shakespeare, prologue to *Henry V*

Traditional ways of learning can teach us a great deal, but what they can never provide is the serendipitous moment in a musty old bookstore when you stumble across the words that set your soul on fire.

Many years ago, on a blustery afternoon in Galway, Ireland, I was meandering through the labyrinthine rooms of Kenny's, the legendary bookstore, when an intriguing book title seized my attention. Down the spine of the book ran the words *In the Chair*. The book was a tantalizing collection of interviews with poets from the North of Ireland. I opened the book at random, in the spirit of the ancient practice of bibliomancy, hoping to find an auspicious line or two to inspire me.

My eyes fell on the words of the great Irish poet, Seamus Heaney, one of the writers who has most deeply influenced me. Speaking about his own rigorous standards, Heaney warned that a writer "shouldn't waver into language" or "tame the strangeness" of his work. The luminous turns in his poems, he says, "are a matter of following on down that road of truth."

He concluded the interview with what he called the famous Dublin triad: "This is it. This is the thing. This is what you're up against."

Who knows why some words ignite the hearts of some readers while others are like wet matches that won't light? Who can say why some words seize the imagination of one reader and not others? Who can say why one person's epiphany is another's cliché?

All I know is that, at that moment, those strangely commanding lines felt mythic, as if they had been written directly to me by an unknown hand. I really had no idea if they were verses from an epic riddle, chants from a battle cry, or some raffish advice Heaney overheard at McDaid's, Dublin's famous literary pub. I only know that they sent a shiver of recognition right through me.

My fingers tingled as I read the words. They had a flint-like quality. They threw off sparks; they ignited the kindling of my imagination. I was transported into the distant past where I could hear the voices of my parents, coaches, mentors, and friends voicing a hundred variations of "No excuses, no alibis, no apologies. Just do what needs to be done *now.*" I'd lived with that sense of urgency. So why did Heaney's words haunt me? Why was I suddenly stricken by "a riot of emotion," in the tumultuous words of Ireland's modern myth-maker, James Joyce?

Suddenly, I knew.

I was stuck. I was lost. I'd lost my fire. Worse, I was waiting, waiting for something to happen, waiting for a miracle, a muse, a breakthrough.

By that time, in early 2001, I'd been blessed with some success, publishing a number of books, shooting many documentary films, and lecturing all over the world. But I'd hit the wall and had the brick marks on my forehead to prove it. I was mired in the quicksand of an unfinished companion book to one of my documentary films, discombobulated about ghosting someone else's book, and confused about how to tell the truth about my own unlived life.

Stuck and, some would say, unfocused—although, if pressed, I preferred the baseball metaphor of just being in a slump. I just hadn't had a hit for a while.

Sure enough, in the strange way of mythic language, Heaney's haunting words seemed to have been written for me, for that moment, for what I was up against. Deceptively simple words, but somehow expressive of my own coiled feelings of amazement and terror. Those three lines reverberated in me like a Celtic *carpe diem*—a reminder to seize the day, live life to the fullest, use time wisely.

As the Roman poet Horace wrote about the mysterious power of mythic language, "Change the name and it's about you." Uncannily, the chance discovery of the incantatory Irish verses drove home to me questions that are perilous to forget: *What are you waiting for? Why are you avoiding the real work? What will it take for you to go deeper?*

What I heard that day in Galway was an echo of the secret struggle I'd been engaged in from the time I was a skinny, idealistic sixteen-year-old cub reporter for my hometown newspaper. Since then, I'd written millions of words and shot thousands of hours of film. But in every one of my projects, I'd gotten as stuck as Brer Rabbit in that nasty old Tar-baby patch. Stuck so often, I realized then and there, standing in the cold Irish rain outside the bookstore, that I hadn't written anything more original than a check or a postcard for months. In the frenzy of life, I'd lost my focus.

All right, I thought. So I'm stuck. I'm lost. I admit it. That's life. I recalled how the maverick mythologist Joseph Campbell confided to me once at the Clift Hotel, in San Francisco, that the essence of the journey is that a hero is *stuck*—and has to get himself *unstuck* or there's no adventure, no story, no art. The point, he added, isn't the agony of the quest, it's the rapture of the revelation. That note from the herald's trumpet meant the world to me.

As I left the bookstore, a soft rain fell over the medieval city. I sauntered past Nora Barnacle's old slate-roofed house, which her husband, James Joyce, visited only once because her parents believed he wrote dirty books. In the town square, I gazed at the statue of Padraic Colum, who spent his life wandering the West Country collecting Irish fairy tales. Fiddle music floated across from Collin's Bar around the corner. I felt a wild surge of joy for the first time in years, a kind of vertigo in the stark beauty that surrounded me.

And then a fugitive line came back to me, as if tossed like a life preserver by my own soul. When the great Tennessee explorer Daniel Boone was asked if he'd ever been lost, he replied, "No, but I was bewildered once for a few days."

My fingers twitched with the old desire to put pen to paper; get some ideas in motion. My mind turned to the warm turf fire in the Connemara cottage where I was staying and it occurred to me that I'd better get home before my own fire went out.

That's the moment this book was born.

THE CIRCULAR ADVENTURE

That day, an image rose in my mind that reminded me of Campbell's idea of the hero's journey. The myriad-minded mythologist, combined the ancient circular symbol of the soul with the eternal wheel of life to create a dynamic image of the search for self-knowledge. For years, I'd kept a sketch of his simple diagram pinned to a corkboard in my writing studio. It helped me visualize the dramatic journey that underwrites movies, novels, and plays. I came to love the adrenaline rush I got from recognizing the three stages of the mythic journey in the three acts of dramatic structure. And on this fateful day in Galway, I recognized in that same iconic voyage the three stages of the *creative* journey.

For over twenty years, I had taught the hero's journey model in Myth and Movie workshops from the American Film Institute to the University of London. I had adapted it as The Pilgrim's Journey for gatherings of spiritual seekers in monasteries and churches, and even as The Business Journey for corporations looking for a competitive edge. The journey model is useful in all these contexts because it offers a clear image of the adventure of self-knowledge, the mystery of change, and the promise of transformation. But until that storm-clouded day in Galway, I hadn't recognized it as a road map for the adventure of creativity.

For millennia, the circle has been the symbol for the Great Round of life. Philosophers, writers, and artists from Aristotle to Robert Frost have considered its power. Van Gogh wrote to his brother, "Life is probably round." Chuang Tsu also comes to mind, "At the still point in the center of the circle one can see the infinite in all things." Around and around we go on the circular journey. Filmmaker David Lynch sees every movie as a circular movement; choreographer Twyla Tharp uses overlapping circles to chart the progress of her ongoing projects. Albert Einstein considered the circle an immortal image. Years ago in an interview I did with beloved religion historian Huston Smith for our book, *The Way Things Are,* he mused, "[T]here is something magical about a circle. For one thing it is geometric; it can encompass more space than any other shape. But this is more than just mathematical. It is also symbolic. A circle travels without leave-taking. So it combines a journeying with a center." Finally, painter Francis Picabin mused, "Our heads are round so that thoughts can change direction." My revelation in the Galway bookstore showed me that the "center" he described could be *my* center and *your* center, and that the journey he referred to could be the long, hard journey of creativity. In turn, being stuck creatively means you're caught in a *vicious* circle and must turn around and try another way.

The English art critic Herbert Read, writing of Paul Klee in his book *The Meaning of Art,* observed, "The artist must penetrate to the source of the life force, the power-house of all time and space, and only then will he have the energy and freedom to create with the proper technique a vital work of art." For Brenda Ueland, that "source of the life force" is always the artist. "There is only one *you*," she wrote. "Consequently, if you speak or write from yourself you cannot help being original. So remember two things: you are talented and you are original." The moral is we must learn to say something new, from the center, from our core, as honestly as possible. If we do so, we can't help but be original; it may not be great, but at least it will be original. That's all we can ever hope to control.

Igniting your creative fire requires focus. And it takes practice, *focused* practice—determined practice of the thing you love until you do it right, until it becomes natural, a habit, a way to conduct yourself. "I believe we learn by practice," said Martha Graham. "Whether it means to learn to dance by practicing dancing or to learn to live by practicing living,

Fire Within, oil on canvas. Self portrait by Laila Carlson, 2007.

the principles are the same." This takes great resolve; it also requires the ability to imagine what you do before you do it. This is harder than it sounds; it requires a leap of faith, a respect for the utter mystery of creativity. Fortunately, great spirits from Lao Tzu to Antoine de Saint-Exupéry, Willa Cather, and Fred Astaire have partly demystified the process for us by telling us how to begin. *Take the first step*. And then take the next step and the one after that. If you take enough steps, it's called a journey.

THE JOURNEY

Imagine the wheel of time turning in a seemingly endless round, revealing that the beginning is the end of another beginning. This is the cyclic nature of the inward journey of creativity, which is by nature *back and down*—back in time and down into the soul's depths. Its endless line suggests infinity, the way time moves, becoming and passing, symbolizing unity, perfection, and eternal progress. This is the archetypal circle that inspired Joseph Campbell's famous model of the hero's journey. Which he divided into three stages: separation, initiation, and return. By contrast, this book will focus on a journey that changes direction—a journey that goes *backward, against* time, *against* the grain. All that *againstness* is a visceral way to describe the overwhelming resistance of the universe to your attempt to do anything original. This is called the left-hand path. This is not the demonic path of superstition, but *widdershins*—literally "against the journey"—reflecting the tension of the real adventure that poet-essayist Edward Hirsch calls in

The Demon and the Angel, "the downswerve into darkness and the unknown."

Now, imagine this path as a spiral and you'll see the path of the creative journey—that yearning for self-expression and fierce need that finds satisfaction only in your creative efforts. The choice is yours. You create or you die. You either take that first step, or you are stuck. Your task in life is to express yourself—to make a mark, as boldly, honestly, and as often as you can. You have to stoke your creative fire, keep it alive long enough to make something that expresses you and then learn to pass it on to others who are reaching out for the torch. You either strike the flint and light the fire, or remain passive and go cold.

At the core of this book is my passionate conviction that, if you long to live a life of purpose and meaning, you must have a creative vision. Then you have to *visualize* the progress of your work if you intend to complete it. Like an actor who rehearses lines or an athlete who mentally pre-plays a game, the more you *imagine* the various stages of your journey, the greater the chances of completing your creative work. Your imagination gives you the courage to keep going if you're stuck, the strength to go deeper if your work isn't bold enough, and the confidence to overcome confusion about where you really and truly are. I believe that looking at your creative process as a journey with a beginning, middle, and end gives you a longer and more realistic view than you normally have.

This book offers a deceptively simple model to help guide you on your creative journey. Its unconventional form blends my own stories from four decades of freelance writing and film work, with my reflections from thirty years of teaching creativity in various forms, and with interviews, anecdotes, and exercises. Throughout the book, you'll be asked three questions: What kind of mark do you want to make? What kind of contribution do you want to make? Why do you do what you do and not something else? Ask yourself these questions throughout your creative journey. They remind you that you pay a hefty price for refusing the call to the creative life. Wasting your time may make you feel anxious, but wasting your talent is like letting your soul rust.

I happily offer this book as a creative road map filled with signposts and milestones to help guide you on your own creative adventure. You can start from the beginning and read it cover-to-cover, open it serendipitously, or focus on the stage of the journey you're most concerned about right now. It depends on where you're stuck and if you want to go deeper with your work. The good news is that the journey is thoroughly known; the tough news is you still have to find your own way. But I can only strike the flint; you must fan the flame. You've got to gather your own "firewood," as David Lynch calls his movie research, and decide if it's worth the effort to move on with your creative work. If that work is vitally important to you—and I hope it is—think of this book as a kind of old-fashioned tinderbox filled with flints, paper, and matches to help you ignite your creative fires. Every image, story, poem, and exercise is included here for one reason—to spark your work. I promise you that everything here has actually fired my own imagination or proved helpful to someone whose work startles and inspires me. But you still have to learn how to stoke your own fire.

Innumerable parallels have been drawn over the centuries between nature's fire and the fire in our souls. Ralph Waldo Emerson's astonishing words come to mind: "Genius is the power for lighting your own fire." If you believe, as I do, that creativity isn't a luxury, but a necessity—a means of survival—then you must ask yourself some fundamental questions before you go on. How important is it for you to express yourself? How badly do you need to leave a mark, to say what's really happened in your life? How critical is it for you to finish what you've started? If it isn't as important as breathing, maybe that's why you're stuck.

One of our wisest little philosophers, Charlie Brown, muses: "Sometimes I lie awake at night and I ask, 'Why am I here?'" In the next panel, a spectral voice answers: "Why? Where do you want to be?'" And that's the key question for you as well. Where do you want to be *creatively?*

On one hand, to create is the most natural thing in the world. One of the characteristics that makes us human is that we are reflective *creators* rather than instinctive *creatures*. To create means to make something new, original, fresh, and vital. The very origins of the word go back to the Latin *creare*, "to grow, to make order out of the chaos," revealing the depths of this irrepressible impulse. But being creative can also feel like the most unnatural endeavor in the world because of the often painful sacrifices of time, money, health, and sometimes sanity it requires.

The breakthrough comes when you realize that not to create is not to grow, not to emerge out of chaos, which, as psychologists remind us, is to court neurosis. When you make

Ravenous (Prometheus) Creates a Human, etching. Copyright © 2005 by Dave Alber.

the bold effort to lead a creative life, you must seize the fire, as Prometheus did when he sparked the very origins of art and culture.

But what if your fire is not burning well or, worse, has gone out? Without inner fire, you have no light, no heat, no desire. You can't move forward without spiritual energy. You may be procrastinating or feeling lazy and unmotivated. You may be distracted by money or relationship problems. Or your creative block just may be a blip from your soul's Early Warning System that you're headed for disaster with your current plans or somehow self-sabotaging your vision.

Regardless, there's only one way out—and that's *through* the dark woods.

You must change your life.

STEPPING ONTO THE PATH

"Step by step, a path; stone by stone, a cathedral," my great-grandfather used to say. I think those are words to live by.

So here it is, in a nutshell. We create or we die. We make a mark or we leave a void. Our task in life is to find our deep soul work and throw ourselves headlong into it. "There's only one way to begin to work," Eugene O'Neill wrote in *Long Day's Journey into Night,* "and that's to get to work." If you burn with the blue desire to begin, there's no time to waste. There is no better time. "Start anywhere," says Cormac McCarthy. There will never be a perfect moment when the stars are aligned, the money is in the bank, the kids are out of the house, and the muses are just a speed-dial away. What's important is to commit to your own creative process. The journey is about making time and space to make your art.

Think about where you want to be a year from now, five years, ten years from now. Consider what you have to do to reach that goal. Put skin and bones on that dream creature called your creative vision. If you believe, along with Doc, the soulful marine biologist in John Steinbeck's *Cannery Row,* that "We have to make a mark, even if it's only a scribble," then it's time to make yours and not worry about success, or fame, or riches.

Are you up to the challenge? Are you going to be a reproduction or an original? Will you strive to be innovative or imitative? Are you ready to take your turn on the page, turn up the heat, turn it on? "Wanna make something out of it?" as we used to taunt on the streets of Detroit. "Do you want to make something out of yourself?" as Roger Turner, my first

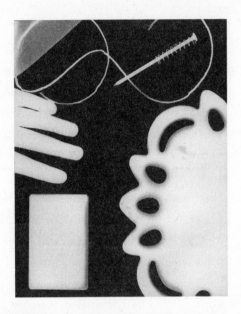

Silhouettes. **Sunprint by Jack Cousineau, 2005.**

newspaper editor, used to challenge me. Are you ready to create something that enlivens and enlarges your world and—if it's got the real fire—ours too?

"A musician must make music," wrote Abraham Maslow, "an artist must paint, a poet must write, if he is to be ultimately at peace with himself. What a man can be, he must." In that spirit, the creative journey is the one you *can't* not take, the work you *can't* not do. But it takes courage to live boldly, a bold heart to become yourself. If you're stuck, you must *move*. To fuel the journey, to rekindle your love of the work, to make this leap of faith requires extraordinary energy. For creativity *is* love's work. If you don't love it, it won't work. And if it won't work, then it's time to stoke the fire.

One night, not long ago, as I was finishing this book, I awoke at dawn with a start. A peculiar dreamline hovered in my mind: "There is a reason you're creative for a reason." I have no idea what this means, other than it's a message from my very soul that there is more meaning and purpose to my fierce desire to make works of art than I'd ever imagined. I don't have to understand why, but I do have to believe in the creative spark that burns within me.

WHERE ARE YOU NOW ON THE CREATIVE JOURNEY?

Where do you want to be?

What will it take to stoke your fire?

PART I

Inspiration

And then there is inspiration. Where does it come from? Mostly from the excitement of living. I get it from the diversity of a tree or the ripple of the sea, a bit of poetry, the sighting of a dolphin breaking the still water and moving toward me, anything that quickens you to the instant. And whether one would call this inspiration or necessity, I really do not know.

—Martha Graham, *Blood Memories*

Casa Grande Ruins. Infrared photograph by Phil Cousineau, 2006.

Uroboros, medieval symbol of circularity, eternity, and self-knowledge. From Horapollio's *Selecta Hieroglyphica,* 1597.

CHAPTER 1

Fires of the Imagination

*The artist must create a spark before he can make a fire
and before art is born the artist must be ready
to be consumed by the fire of his own creation.*

—Auguste Rodin

Inspiration is a flash of fire in the human soul. Consider the marvel: the inrush of spirit, the flash of an idea, the flame of insight, the spark of imagination. It's the *Aha, Eureka,* and *Hallelujah* moment all rolled into one. Inspiration is a message-in-a-bottle from the distant shore, a window into the other world, a tap of the muse's finger, the grace of the gods. It comes when you least expect it, when your defenses are down and your vulnerability up. It arrives in a dream, a conversation, a brainstorm—and leaves without warning.

Inspiration is John Coltrane emerging out of a four-day silence with *Love Supreme* streaming through his soul. It's Pierre Bonnard running to the easel after seeing his wife bathed in golden light in their bathtub. It's Paul McCartney drifting off to sleep one night with the words "everyone lives in a yellow submarine" floating through his head. It's the *New Yorker* cartoon with the light bulb flashing over the head of the starry-eyed inventor.

Inspiration can also feel like a sudden possession. The mass hypnosis that came over Michelangelo and a group of fellow sculptors in Rome the day the Greek sculpture *Laocoon* was lifted out of the ground is illustrative of this fantastic aspect of inspiration, because it immediately compelled the entire group to draw it.

Sometimes softly, sometimes violently, sometimes sweetly, inspiration swoops down and *compels* us to express ourselves, the devil be damned. Suddenly, we're moved to speak our minds, like the ecstatic Chinese poet Li Po, who believed he was divinely inspired to write his travel poems and drinking songs; or Jane Austen, who was determined to write even after being banished to a tiny desk in the cramped hallways of the family home; or Rembrandt, who resorted to painting dozens of self-portraits when he ran out of money for models.

If inspired, the creative spirit takes wing, soars, surprises, blazes with radiance. "The glow of inspiration warms us," Ovid wrote 2000 years ago, "and it is a holy rapture." Allen Ginsberg said, "I write poetry because the English word *inspiration* comes from Latin, *spiritus*, breath, and I want to breathe freely." "Who knows where it came from?" French philosopher Maurice Merleau-Ponty admits, "My own words take me by surprise and teach me what to think." Singer Ani DiFranco sighs, "I have no idea where it comes from. It isn't fair."

Inspiration: it's fascinating, enchanting, angrifying, exasperating, and elusive. If you try to pin it down, it squirms like Proteus, the Greek god of shapeshifting. It mocks your attempts to capture it with ropes of theory, keeping its secrets by slip-sliding away from you. If you deny it altogether and try to will your work into being without it, the work is recognized as "uninspired"—possibly the worst critique you can receive, because it insinuates you're mechanical, soulless. On the other hand, trying to force yourself to "be inspired" is like trying to think more clearly by squinting.

What you *can* do is be ready when the moment comes to work. You can be receptive, ready, and audacious.

Stephen King's *On Writing* is one of the best no-nonsense guides to the creative process in years. In it, he writes: "Let's get one thing clear right now, shall we? There is no Idea Dump, no Story Central, no Island of the Buried Bestsellers; good ideas seem to come from literally nowhere, sailing at you right out of the empty sky . . . Your job isn't to find these ideas but to recognize them when they show up."

So inspiration may be an unpredictable friend, as inscrutable as an oracle and fickle as a weathervane. But if you're serious about your own creativity, you have no choice but to try to make it . . . well . . . *scrutable,* to salvage a wonderful old word. What you can do is improve the odds that your spirit will be *moved* by being alert to whatever form inspiration may take.

The recurring theme reflected in my own various passions—from the arts, to politics, to the spiritual life, to architecture, to baseball—is the ardent belief that the sparks of inspiration are everywhere. If I remain open to the wild fire they portend and don't hide behind the shutters of cynicism, sooner or later, one will ignite. In some still-elusive way, inspiration has to be both *everywhere* and *everywhen*, because it isn't a luxury for me. It's not a hobby; it's my life. Everything has to fit, sooner or later, into my insatiable desire to be creative or it feels like my life is backfiring.

For me, this means that I find inspiration in the rainbow flight of wild parrots over our house in San Francisco, the bells tolling from the church down the hill, the laughter of nursery-school kids walking in the rain, the lived-in face of an old Filipino newspaper seller, and the chance 1930s postcard stuck into one of my father's books. If I'm stuck, I look far and wide for the fires that will kindle my inspiration. My life revolves around this constant search. If I'm not on fire, I'm not inspired, and I can't work. If I force it, the work always sounds as if it's written in someone else's voice.

When asked what inspires me, I say, "Whatever sets my soul on fire." That means travel, books, art, music, photographs, nature, or café conversation. Often as not, it's the ordinary wonders that do it—the sandal-maker, the mail carrier, or a *cantoneiro,* a sidewalk tile-setter I met in Lisbon years ago who felt he'd been given a gift from God in his ability to lay tile in beautiful, swirling black-and-white patterns.

As I knelt to watch him work, I saw a glint in his eye that revealed devotion to his craft and gratitude for the gift he'd been given. That inner light has shone on in me till this day.

To immerse myself in the extraordinary, I seek out the paintings of Bonnard, the symphonies of Mahler, the sculptures of Henry Moore, the nature essays of Annie Dillard, the plays of Eugene O'Neill, the poetry of Philip Levine, the songs of Van Morrison, the slick lines of a '64 Mustang, and the lilt in my son's voice when he says, "Pop." And I can't live without my daily dose of creative fire. Without it, I become neurotic—or grumpy, as my son tells me. But at least I know I'm not alone in this fierce desire. Seven hundred years ago Rumi told his followers: "Make friends with your burning." Fifty years ago, jazz great Miles Davis was so lit up by Charlie Parker's he cried out, "I want his fire!"

However, *caveat lector*. Reader, beware. There are at least two kinds of inspiration. The first lifts your spirit, as spirituals and sunsets do. It makes you feel good, which isn't bad. But the second lifts your spirit and then flings you like a flaming arrow, full of passion and resolve to set the world on fire. This is the *duende,* the dark song in the gypsy soul, the black light that enflames the canvas, the spark that enlarges the heart. This is the blood surge that can be detected in the poems of Federico Lorca, the paintings of Edvard Munch, and the dances of Martha Graham. And it's combustible.

In this sense, inspiration is a gift from the back of beyond—a revelation of what separates us from all other species. We are moved to create, not out of brute instinct or biological necessity, but because we feel something so deeply we *must* respond, however carefully. Tchaikovsky describes this formidable force, in a letter dated from Florence, Italy, February 17 (March 1) 1878:

> *If that condition of mind and soul which we call inspiration lasted long without intermission, no artist could survive it. The strings would break and the instrument be shattered into fragments. It is already a great thing if the main ideas and general outline of a work come without any racking of brains, as the result of that supernatural and inexplicable force we call inspiration.*

This isn't just shoveling smoke. It has everything to do with striving to express something—not off the top of your head, but from your fiery depths. Olympic gymnast Mary Lou Retton put it this way: "Each of us has a fire in our hearts for something. It's our goal in life to find it and keep it lit." This goes for superb athletes, great artists, and also for rice farmers in the Philippines, brick-layers in Guatemala, teachers in Buffalo, and nurses in the Scottish Highlands. They can all teach you something about how to stoke the fires even under the harshest circumstances.

I'm trying to tell you something important here. The creative urge matters. Stories matter. Images matter. It matters that you were born with a genius, a guiding spirit, a daimon that may know more about your destiny than you do. It matters that there's an abyss between human hearts that can be bridged with ink, paint, stone, and music. It matters which words you use to bridge that chasm. "Stories," "sparks," "fires," "genius," "daimon," "heart" are all sacred words in my vocabulary, because they do just that. But words aren't enough. You need something more, a spur that quickens you into action, a trigger that makes the phoenix in you rise from its ashes. You must make these words and desires move; you need to move beyond inspiration until it becomes something else.

The great Oregon poet William Stafford speaks of a mythic thread of destiny woven by the Three Fates: "There's a thread you follow. It goes among / Things that change. But it doesn't change . . . "When in doubt about what you're supposed to be doing with your fierce heart, think about this thread. Is it your faith in the divine, your love of family, your vocation as a creative artist or entrepreneur? In this book, I will try to convince you to hold onto that thread as you enter the dark labyrinth of your incomplete work, no matter what your motivation.

HOLD ONTO THE THREAD

This much I know. The creative journey is a search for the *deeply* real. It's a fiery attempt to make real some idea, some vision that is uncomfortably *un*real until it's created. The search for inspiration, like Stafford's mythic thread, is never-ending. The thread is the force that makes you real—if you don't let go of it. Your work will never be real—realized—until you are.

Here is a very real description of inspiration given by ten-year-old Nila Devaney, from Arcata, California:

Inspiration is foolish. He doesn't lie, but he only begins the truth. He is the one who starts the picture and completes the world. Without inspiration, there would not be you. Inspiration is like a candle: the flame of everything, the start of everything. Every time inspiration walks into a new neighborhood, he immediately makes friends with the kids.

Ah, from the mouths of babes.

I'm fascinated by those of any age and talent whose spirit has been awakened by this depth of awe and wonder. But I also know that, at the end of the day, it's up to me to pick up the pen or the camera. Over the years, I've learned to respect the deceptively simple wisdom behind folk stories about creativity—like the wonderful legend from China in which an old king gold-plates his bathtub and commands his finest craftsmen to carve upon it fine sayings from the old sages. Each morning during his bath, the king meditates on these sayings, which he called the Five Excellent Practices, in order to rule as wisely as possible.

The next three chapters explore the first three stages on the creative journey: celebrating the waking dream of reverie, having the courage to seize the moment, and seeking the wisdom of those who can help you *make* what you once only *imagined*. Each chapter offers a handful of "excellent practices" or exercises you can use to activate your imagination and stir the creative fire smoldering inside you. As Yogi Berra described baseball practice, "There are deep depths there."

The Roman writer Pliny the Elder cites Cicero as the origin of one of my favorite expressions:

> *Whilst they as Homer's Iliad in a nut,*
> *A world of wonders in one closet shut.*

The verse refers to an ancient practice in which scribes copied Homer's great epic in script so tiny all 17,000 verses could fit inside a walnut shell. Soldiers could then carry the book into battle for inspiration, as Alexander is believed to have done when he marched to India.

FIRES OF THE IMAGINATION IN A NUTSHELL

Your imagination holds news of eternity. Inspiration comes and goes, creativity is the result of practice. There is a gold thread from your soul to your real work. Hold onto it for dear life. There is a force within you that breathes divine fire and brings your work to life. Honor it at all costs. Give us something the world's never seen before: *you*.

WHERE ARE YOU *NOW*
ON THE CREATIVE JOURNEY?

How will you turn inspiration into aspiration?

What will it take for imagination to catch fire?

Faded Angel. Photograph by Joanne Warfield, 2007.

CHAPTER 2

Celebrating Reverie

*Psychically speaking, we are created by our reverie—created
and limited by our reverie—for it is the reverie which
delineates the furthest limits of the mind . . . We have not
experienced something until we have dreamed it.*

—Gaston Bachelard, *Poetics of Reverie*

March 1986. Late Saturday night, sipping cappuccino in the
old Café Figaro in L.A. I picked up a newspaper and turned to
the movie section. My eyes fell upon a curious photograph. It
was unmistakably a portrait of Napoleon—but it was carved
out of a grain of rice and inserted into the eye of a needle.

After giving the image the old "once-over-twice,"
I learned from the caption that it was the work of a Soviet-
Armenian émigré, a "micro-miniature sculptor," by the name
of Hagop Sandaldjian, whose first exhibition was opening that

night at a local gallery. I couldn't resist the sly wink of synchronicity. This I had to see for myself.

Later that night, I found myself eyeing the strangely amusing photographs of Sandaldjian's creations on the gallery wall. The exhibition catalogue described the artist as a virtuoso viola player and an ergonomics expert who had learned his miniscule art from a fellow Slavic musician. When he came to America in the seventies, he settled in L.A., but had difficulty finding steady work. Eventually, he began to create what one critic described as his "unimaginably minute worlds within the eye of a needle."

When my turn came to lean over and peer into one of the microscopes, I felt myself falling, as if down a slippery slope of metal tubing. At first, I saw nothing but the gauzy reflection of the inside of my own eyelid. Then the gallery walls seemed to close in; my head felt like smoke and my hands like ashes. I groped for the focus knob and twisted it until the image of Napoleon standing on a pedestal appeared, his hand thrust inside his black overcoat. Dazzled, I moved on to the next microscope. This one revealed a grain of rice on which was spelled out in Arabic: "There is no God but Allah, and Mohammed is his Prophet." Next came rice grains featuring Mount Ararat, reputed home of Noah's Ark, and an image of Donald Duck made from the dust of crushed diamonds and rubies.

The Lilliputian artwork took my breath away, which is no throwaway phrase. Japanese calligraphers are known to wait for the moment between heartbeats before putting brush to paper. Sandaldjian cultivated the same discipline, waiting

above: **Hagop Sandaldjian creating his micro-miniature sculptures. Museum of Jurassic Technology.**

right: Baseball! **Sandaldjian's micro-ballplayer installed on the edge of a needle, 1970s.**

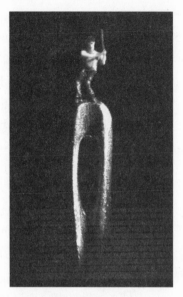

for the nanosecond *between his pulses* before cutting into the delicate rice grains—a length of time that's been deftly named the "creative pause" by Magda Proskauer, a teacher of breathing techniques.

While gazing in amused awe at Sandaldjian's creation of a miniscule left-handed baseball hitter with a red cap, I overheard a professorial man say that those who'd witnessed the artist at work claim they couldn't tell when his hands moved. He appeared to be in a reverie, lost in a wondrous world of his own making. Looking up from the microscope, I had the sense of swooping back into my body, a sense that I'd encountered the work of someone who'd reached into the holy fire of the creative spirit. As Bill Cosby says, "I only told you that story to tell you this one."

Driving back to my hotel in Westwood, I was overcome by the reeling sense that *transportive* art always provides me. I felt as if I'd been gone for a long time, in a strange land. No doubt about it, the planet is bulging with artwork. But *numinous* art is rare, like the long-lost bronze statue of a victorious charioteer hauled up from the bottom of the Mediterranean. When we encounter what's been conceived in fire, the flames spread and we're set ablaze by the revelation of another world. We're inspired, but not out of fawning admiration. We're moved by the enchantment, the effort that moves us to what St. Therese called "the tenderness that moves words to action," and the emotion that brings us close to whatever is divine in life.

The Armenian virtuoso's work was more than impressive. It was *compelling*. It goaded me into looking at the world in a new way, like the magic mirrors held up by human hands in Jean Renoir's masterpiece, *Beauty and the Beast,* that forced Beauty to look at herself as she floated down the hallway. All great works, those infused with the soul of the artist, feel haunting because they seem to *look back* at you. They provoke you into asking yourself questions you've been avoiding. In the strange alchemy of art, Sandaldjian's work sparked a desire in me to work, to *make something of my own.*

Later that night, as a scepter moon hung over the towering palm trees in the hotel courtyard and oranges fell softly into the pool, I was alternately riddled with awe and addled with self-loathing. Disappointment stung like a paper cut. I couldn't sleep. I had to wonder if I'd ever done anything with the precision and patience revealed by the sculptor's preternaturally steady hands. I drifted in and out of reverie, writing spidery notes to myself in a big black journal—random thoughts about what I wanted to accomplish before I died, books I vowed to write, and distant lands I swore I'd visit.

Waking up the next morning, I wondered who'd snuck into my room while I was sleeping and written in my journal—in my own handwriting! Rereading the entries, I realized it wasn't enough anymore to be working on other people's projects, no matter how hip or well paid. Co-writing, editing, researching the kaleidoscopic sixties were all fun, but they didn't reflect enough of *my* voice, *my* world. I needed to tell *my* stories, release the daemon—or demon—that was lurking in me and clawing to get out.

That's the beauty of reverie. It allows your mind to meander until the truth outs. It emboldens you to do the work you didn't know you'd been dreaming about—or had been assiduously avoiding. Sometimes it just takes a little nudge to move you where you ought to be. Sometimes it requires a spark to set off an explosion that prevents the earthquake of frustration. It's the creative work that keeps you from going crazy. The first step on the creative journey must be to recognize when the *peculiar mood* of reverie is upon you—those strange conditions that enable the unfolding of the creative process. This is why reverie is the first fire that must be stoked.

THE RIVER OF REVERIE

The French philosopher Gaston Bachelard is the poet laureate of reverie. To my lights, he is one of the most sublime writers of the 20th century. In *Poetics of Reverie,* he wrote that reverie holds the capacity to exalt life and helps us to "inhabit . . . the world of happiness." Tantalizingly, he adds, "If the dreamer had 'the gift,' he would turn his reverie into a work."

That's the key, the trigger, the tipping or turning point. If you've ever been deeply moved by the feeling of a waking dream—perhaps at a great play or opera, on a canyon river, witnessing a child opening a birthday present, or as I was by Sandaldjian's oneiric creations—then you know what it means to fall down the sweet slope of reverie. With its roots in the soul of the dreamer, reverie is a gift from below, the opportunity to dream with your eyes open. As Bachelard writes, in some ineffable way, we actually seem to be *defined* by our reveries, even created by them.

To describe the waking dream demands something more than everyday language; the effort calls for words that, as many of us have suspected, cast a spell—words like "trance," "delirium," or "levitate"—tumultuous words that help describe the indescribable when we feel as if we've fallen through a trapdoor into another mood, or been lifted into another world.

"When in doubt, look it up," my dad used to say. Though he's been gone for twenty years, the touch of his hand is still there on my shoulder, edging me toward my *Oxford Unabridged Dictionary*. Riffling through its pages, I discover that "reverie" is an early 17th-century French word for "rejoicing" and "revelry." Later, I summoned Mr. Webster and found: "a daydream, a delirium, the condition of being lost in thought." These worlds within words help me appreciate reverie even more.

But for me, the million-dollar question is how to turn the waking dream into the *working* dream. I've spent half my life tantalized by the possibility of *consciously* stoking the fires of reverie. Over the years, I've searched for compelling stories about creative people who lived for reverie, such as the painter Jean Arp whose ideal was to paint so others could view his work as he painted it, as if dreaming with their eyes open. I've wondered if we are on the verge of an evolutionary leap forward, as novelist Henry Miller believed: "The art of dreaming awake will be in the power of every man one day." I've reveled in eccentric characters like Gérard de Nerval, who walked his purple lobster in the Luxembourg Gardens to prolong his hypnagogic reveries. And I doff my hat to comedian Steven Wright who describes the uncanniness of life as well as any phenomenologist: "I fell asleep in a neighbor's satellite dish and my dreams were seen on televisions all over the world."

With her trademark rhythms and rhymes, the glorious Emily Dickinson tells us that "revery" is an essential component in the creation of nature itself.

> To make a prairie it takes a clover and one bee,
> One clover, and a bee, and revery.
> The revery alone will do, if bees are few.

By extension, at the heart of our nature is the capacity for creativity, which likewise requires the self-luminous waking dream. It is in this state of spiritual readiness that creative souls sense the pull of destiny.

The history of art is crowded with creative people willing to do whatever it took to help them climb Jacob's Ladder—that age-old symbol of aspiration and revelation. For Marcel

Proust, the taste of a simple cookie was enough to slingshot him back to childhood and then back to the present, a dream journey that inspired his epic novel *In Search of Lost Time*. Constantin Brâncuşi caressed woodcarvings he carried all the way from his homeland of Romania and read his native folk tales to reanimate his sculptures. In turn, English sculptress Barbara Hepworth visited Brâncuşi's studio to encounter the "miraculous feeling of eternity mixed with beloved stone and stone dust" and to feel the "inspiration of a dedicated workshop." Honoré de Balzac sniffed rotten apples he kept in his desk drawer to evoke the wretched smells of the medieval Paris about which he wrote. Stephen Hawking, the wheelchair-bound physicist, revels in the long stretch of time it takes him to get into bed each night to mull over the days unsolved science problems. Joanne Shenandoah walks through the woods of the Onondaga reservation listening to the voices of her ancestors.

left: Jacob's Dream (Le rêve de Jacob), **Old Testament engraving.**

opposite: **Barbara Hepworth sculpture garden, Cornwall, England. Photograph by Phil Cousineau, 1980.**

Think about what helps you slip into reverie, then find ways to keep it present in your life.

Since childhood, I've devised ways to slip into daydreams, knowing I couldn't afford to wait for inspiration to "strike." On of my earliest memories is hearing my best friend's mother discourage him from taking me too seriously because I was nothing but a daydreamer. All my life, I've gazed off into space, irking my parents, teachers, and friends. I sit and stare, walk and gaze, and do everything I can to stretch my dreams out as long as possible—in a hot shower, in the morning with the paper, at the bakery, on newly cut grass, listening to the chatter of kids playing baseball. Whenever I get a spark, I do what I can to keep it alive, fanning the flames until they roar—writing it down, sketching it, singing it, learning it by heart, or talking it out with friends and family. I'm happy to say it's an ancient urge.

EXERCISE 1: *First, dream the painting, then, paint the dream.* Van Gogh's revelation to his brother about the role of reverie is a spark off the flint for your own work.

At random, pick a book off your bookshelf.

Open it and choose a line or two. Learn the words by heart or write them down on an index card.

Take those words "out for a walk," as Paul Klee said about drawing. Write about them without thinking, as fast as you can, for two minutes. Surprise yourself.

Fold the paper or card and carry it with you for the rest of the day. Let the words lead you away into the land of reverie.

Do this every day until it's a habit.

FROM REVERIE TO CREATIVITY

When Navajo sculptor Nora Naranjo-Morse wants to make her beautiful clay vessels, she drives out to a riverbed her mother showed her when she was a child. "When I come here I'm excited, I'm like a child," she says in Michael Apted's brilliant documentary film, *Inspirations*.

> *Nothing can hurt me. No one is going to say anything mean to me here. Everything is so peaceful, and beautiful, and perfect, so I just open up. That's exactly what we're supposed to do; that's exactly what I'm looking for when I'm going to create,*

*that I'm opening up. I'm opening up to this force
that I'm not afraid of and that I can just let myself
fall into and be inspired. I think about the people
I love, and think about the things around me so
that when I go back to my home and my studio I
carry this with me and I'm able to create and open
up again and let it all flow into those vessels I'm
making.*

For Nora and many other indigenous people I've known, the "where" in question doesn't refer to a physical place as much as metaphysical one. Their focus and reverence is on the heightening of spiritual sensibilities, the celebration of the Great Mystery.

"It's all about reverie," says Gregg Chadwick, a visionary oil painter from Southern California. He told me in a recent conversation that, "I need some kind of *flight* if I'm going to create on the canvas what I see in my head. To get that effect, I need to capture a kind of timelessness and leave the mystery of the world between memory and dream intact."

Over the last decade, Chadwick's work has been inspired by his years crisscrossing Southeast Asia as the son of a career military officer. There, his eyes were opened to the intersecting paths of art, music, literature, and religion. His paintings of Buddhist monks and temples and the accelerating pace of life explore the ephemeral aspects of reality. His most profound challenge is offering his viewers an opportunity to be as *transported* as he is when he paints. "I have to get into a special mood to create the *art* and not just *product*. So I'm very careful about the music I play, what's hanging on the walls of my studio, the books stacked in the corner, what I've been eating that morning, even conversations with my son." His work springs from a fierce soul-struggle, living proof that, if you want to be original, you have to learn to trust your reveries, your voice, your vision, and resist the temptation of style and fashion. Otherwise you'll never, as Bob Marley sang so thrillingly, "Satisfy your soul."

"What if," Coleridge wondered, "in your dream you went to heaven and there plucked a strange and beautiful flower? And what if, when you woke, you had the flower in your hand? Ah! What then?" In the spring of 2002, P. J. Curtis, a Dublin DJ and music producer, told me a strange story in an old country pub in County Clare. His aunt had so many dreams in which she heard "fairy music" that she took to keeping a pencil tied to her bedpost so she could write down the music in the middle of the night. By the time she died, the wallpaper in her bedroom was festooned with musical notation from her dreams, some of which was eventually recorded by famed Irish groups like the Chieftains and the Dubliners.

Amazing grace, we might say. But the rational mind cries out: What's happening here? In *Lifetide*, biologist Lyall Watson attempts an explanation: "Hieronymus Bosch and William Blake did it visually, Samuel Taylor Coleridge and James Joyce managed it with words. They succeeded in diverting the stream of consciousness in ways that allowed dream imagery to survive in the harsh light of day . . . We do it every time we daydream."

The trick is to make the dream come alive. To do that, we have to "make something out of it." We don't truly know ourselves until we put our experiences into words or images with love and abandon.

EXERCISE 2. Six Ways to Dream with Your Eyes Open

Write down a morning dream. Keep it alive all day. Think about it at breakfast, in the car, at the café, until it inspires a response. Now make something out of it, a song, a poem, a story, a weaving, a mosaic.

Go to an art museum. Pick one painting. Look at it until you see it. Walk around inside it. Lose yourself in it. Imagine you're the artist. Re-create it in your mind so you can always conjure it when in need of inspiration.

Spring open a long-locked trunk. Strong smells and old possessions transport us; they catalyze memory and summon the muses. Let them trigger a story.

Focus and relax. William Wordsworth's secret trick for inspiring himself was concentrating on one thing, then turning away with what he called "soft eyes," relaxing, until whatever he saw became beautiful.

Spend a day blindfolded. Martial arts legend Bruce Lee practiced his hardest moves with a bandana over his eyes until he could see, he said, with his inner eyes.

Read to children. It sets their hearts on fire and rekindles your own. Remember that *The Hobbit* sprang out of a single line from J.R.R. Tolkien's "Winter Reads," his improvised stories to his own kids. "In a hole in the ground there lived a hobbit . . ."

WHAT THEN SHALL WE DO?

For R. B. Morris, a prolific singer, songwriter, and playwright from Knoxville, Tennessee, reverie is a subtle but powerful trigger. Recently he explained why:

> *It's the starting point for me, the threshold of creativity. It's the moment where all your other mental and physical functions fold into "dreamy thinking or imagining," as Webster's says, "fanciful musing, a visionary notion." If we really want to cultivate our creativity, we simply need to schedule our lives around the production of reverie. Frankly, I have to declare myself severely undisciplined in matters of creativity, but I do try to move toward those times of day when reverie comes easiest, such as the hours of waking or before sleep. The mind seems more willing then to throw off the harness of the world and allow the otherworldly to emerge. Of course, then one has to cultivate one's own process of observing and taking notes. Still, for all one's cultivation, the muse has a tendency to come and go as she pleases. So it's best to keep pen and paper at hand, even if I'm driving my pickup up on*

the mountain, and be ready to roll with the reverie
whenever it occurs.

You know that a deep chord has been struck in you when a story, an image, a color, a drawn line, a melody taunts you until you figure out why you've been so deeply shaken. Australian director Peter Weir's film, *The Year of Living Dangerously*, did just that to me when it was released over twenty years ago. Rarely a day goes by that I don't hear the voice of actress Linda Hunt, playing a male stringer for a Malaysian newspaper at the time of Sukarno's overthrow, asking plaintively: "What then must we do?" She asks this at the crisis point when she takes a stand for all she believes in, even at the risk of her life. She asks it again and again in a fierce voiceover as her fingers fly across her typewriter keys. The challenging question is taken from Tolstoy's *Confession*, a searing account of his mid-life spiritual crisis when he saw "nothing ahead except ruin." The answer came to him in a voice: "See that you remember." Then he woke up.

With the whole world coming at us like a great thrashing wave, how do we recognize and remember reverie, especially when technology is now doing so much of the recall for us? There's only one trick I know of and it's not really a ruse. Write it down. Beat poet Gary Snyder once told me: "The only difference between writers and everybody else is that we always keep a thirty-nine cent notebook in our pockets. You never know when the inspiration might hit." Many years later, I was startled to hear, in a radio interview with author Anne Rice, that she relied so heavily on daydreams that, for her, writing *is* daydreaming, which sometimes provides coded messages, including entire characters, like the twins in *The Queen of the Damned*. Jorge Borges ardently claimed in his Harvard lecture on craft that all writing is guided dream. Shadowbox artist Joseph Cornell said his work happened in a half-sleep. "Our dreams are a second life," he said, "the overflowing of the dream into real life." Photographer-artist Joanne Warfield tells me that reverie comes to her "in the form of enchantment or trance. I watch thoughts, ideas, and images floating by like leaves on a stream of consciousness. Sometimes when I'm in the midst of creating, reverie appears as inspiration for me to try something innovative—but I have to be alert, which can be hard when you're enchanted."

THREE WAYS TO RECOGNIZE REVERIE:

The shudder: "First a shudder runs through, and then the old awe steals over you," says Plato. Don't be afraid of it. The muse is near.

The shiver: Vladimir Nabokov, in his studies on American Literature, describes the moment of truth as the one that sends a *frisson,* a shiver, up your spine. Trust it.

The amazement: Be amazed by it. Amazement is second cousin to awe, a friend of astonishment. Be wary of the snarky people who mock your love of life, your desire to make art.

HONORING THE FIRE

To take the first step on the path of the creative journey, you must honor any moment that sets your heart on fire, because it's a sign that you've fallen in love with the work. Your creative life depends on it. The life of your imagination swings on the rusty hinge of your commitment to your inward life. The wellspring of your creativity depends on the presence of Eros, the god of love, the archetypal force that brings forth meaning, wisdom, and beauty.

If you're looking for clues to a robust creative life, you can find them in the courage to create out of a sense of unabashed joy. This is Rumi's "secret turning," the slow revolutions in the soul of the dervish, the poet, and the lover that, in turn, turn the universe. It's the "creative breakthrough" that scientist Alan Lightman describes as the moment you finally flash on the answer to a crippling conundrum. And it's the "zest and gusto" that Ray Bradbury says is the prerequisite for honest and impassioned work.

I've had to make these tough turns throughout my career if I wanted to create honest work. When I was stuck on the forty-ninth draft of a story from *The Book of Roads,* set in the Philippines, I had to plunge back into that sultry world by cutting open a mango. The explosion of smell immediately vaulted me back to the rice terraces in Northern Luzon, where I heard the fruit seller singing, "Mango, mango, manggggooooo!" That sensory surge helped me finish the story. To write "Pitch Dark," a baseball poem, I opened my dad's old army trunk and retrieved a box of baseball cards I'd put there many years before. I selected a few cards and was transported back to Tiger Stadium where the poem unfolds. To write about the myth of Sisyphus in *Once and Future Myths,* I clutched a hand-sized marble sculpture of two-faced Janus I had bought for a few drachmas from a farmer near Corinth where Sisyphus reigned as king. To help jolt my imagination for a recent film, *City 21: The Future of Urban Life,* I traveled to Casa Grande, the magnificent Anasazi ruins in Arizona (see page 27) where I could soak in its preternatural beauty and see for myself what the ancient future can teach us about sustainable design.

Once I had accepted each of these invitations to move stealthily into the slipstream between the dreaming and waking worlds where the real work is born, all I had to do was ride the mystery. And then, of course, make it real.

Think about what it takes for you to be inspired. What do you do to cultivate reverie? Have you ever had the feeling that something you've created is *this close* to approximating your vision for it? Are you haunted by the possibility that you still haven't done your best work?

EXERCISE 3: **A One-hour Reverie Exercise**

Hold in your hand an example of the most glorious piece of work in your field—a book, if you're a writer; a painting, if a painter; an architecture model, if an architect; and so on.

"Sense your way into the work," Dutch psychologist Robert Bosnak suggests. Feel your way into it and once inside move around inside it. Try to see your old work with new ideas.

Slowly dream your way into this exemplary work; imagine your own work, signed, sealed and delivered into your own hand. Weigh it, smell it, move it.

Now open your eyes and, like a Polynesian navigator, try to visualize the island you're sailing to, even if it's 2000 miles away.

Write down, sketch, sculpt, weave, compose something in response. Think about this: the Viking bards used to say that a person who has his own fire is the one best equipped for life. This means you have not fully experienced something until you've recreated it, put it into your own words or images.

CELEBRATING REVERIE IN A NUTSHELL

If you want to be more creative, trust your
   waking dreams.
When in doubt, work out of your vivid sense
   memories.
Creativity is the destiny of reverie.

HOW'S YOUR PASSAGE?

Do you feel the secret turning?

What do your reveries want to turn into?

The Liquid Hour, oil on linen by Gregg Chadwick, 1998.

CHAPTER 3

Seizing the Moment

*The soul's answer to the problem of time is the
experience of timeless being. There is no other answer.*

—Jacob Needleman, *Time and the Soul*

In 1967, Marta Becket, a sixty-five-year-old ex-chorus girl,
ballerina, artist, and choreographer, took a holiday from her
chaotic life in New York City and drove cross-country with
her husband to California. Outside of a windblown, borax
mining town formerly called Amargosa and now Death Valley
Junction, they suffered a flat tire. While it was being repaired,
Marta wandered around the town and noticed an abandoned
opera house. "I found my ship out here in the desert when I
was 43, which is a little old," she remembered years later in
the Oscar-nominated film *Amargosa*. "But I thought that this

place was begging for life. It took an hour to decide." Becket spent the next six years repairing the theater and painting new murals, writing plays, choreographing dances, and composing music. At first, she played to a near-empty house. Slowly, word spread about a must-see performer way out in Death Valley—an eccentric, possibly brilliant, woman who danced and sang in her own plays in her own theater. "It was a hard time in the beginning, but I'm still dancing and I'm going to keep moving till I drop . . . I call my talent my best friend. If no audience came at all I'd still perform . . . The audiences didn't come to see 32 pliés. They came to see what I'd created out of what I had."

In *Amargosa*, Ray Bradbury, the maven of science fiction, shakes his head with a mixture of admiration and infatuation. "What she did was a revelation. It brought tears to my eyes. She represented to me the spirit of the individual, the spirit of theater, the spirit of creativity. You think the past is past and maybe tonight I can be the me I always wanted to be." If you want to be an artist, he says, "You just need yourself and the nerve to stand up there. For God's sake, if you want to do a thing, just go do it."

Marta Becket's spirit-surging story is to the world of dance and theater what the story of Ray Kinsella and Shoeless Joe Jackson in *Field of Dreams* is to baseball: "If you build it, they will come." She built it and they came, in droves, out of curiosity about the irrepressible creative spirit. But also, I believe, out of a hidden hope that they too would be sparked. Stories about souls on fire, from eccentric artists to driven athletes, are irresistible. Oddly enough, they remind me of the hypnotic effect that cruise ships have on people walking by the docks and waving to people on deck who are following their own dream to see the world, encouraging them while fantasizing about what would happen if they took a similar risk, seized the moment, followed a dream, and sailed around the world. It's what separates the frivolous fantasy from the well-lived life.

SACRED TIME

I'm intrigued by how people use their time. I suspect half of the secret to the creative process lies there. Everyone with a pulse is inspired sometime, somewhere, but life exacts so many demands on our time, that people rarely hit the brakes and ask life's referee for a "Time out."

Thomas Edison was famous for his inventions, but also for innovations like his "Insomnia Squad," a team that worked in round-the-clock shifts in his laboratory so that somebody would always be awake if a great breakthrough in their research suddenly appeared. "Opportunity is missed by most people," he said, "because it is dressed in overalls and looks like work."

The opening scene of *Dead Poet's Society* captures the essence of our bittersweet relationship with the titanic power of time. A high school literature professor (Robin Williams) enters the story like a latter-day Puck, encouraging his students, in Horace's famous words, to "Seize the day"—*carpe diem*. While working on the book *The Olympic Odyssey,* I discovered that this famous line actually comes from a much older saying from ancient Greece. The original maxim enjoined us to "Seize the moment," in reference to Kairos, the Greek god of sacred time, synchronicity, good timing, the right moment, and opportunity. In contrast to the ordinary time of Chronos (chronological time), *kairos* means holy, sacred, or God-given time. Kairos signals a time of crisis, but also new possibilities, decisive action, a stream of moments. "The sense behind that imperative," says Billy Collins, former Poet Laureate of the United States, "is that we don't have an unlimited number of days."

Recognizing sacred time means acknowledging that the moment to act is now, whether for overarching issues like peace and justice, or for immediate concerns. When you eat or sleep by the clock, you live chronologically; if you eat when you're hungry and sleep when you're tired, you live *kairologically*. To create *only* when you're inspired is to create by the clock; to create when your soul is hungry and sleep when you've exhausted yourself with the work you love is to live and work in sacred time.

This is the way I long to live—*timelessly*. I made a vow that I'd live by my own clock the day I punched the time-clock for the last time at a steel factory in Detroit thirty years ago. Ever since, I've wanted to use my time by living outside it, which, for me, is inside the world of myth, art, and dream. I want my life to catch fire and I want to pass that fire on to others, like the fire of relay torches in the ancient long-distance races. I want to *stretch* time like an India rubber man, and not be its victim.

In *Time and the Art of Living*, Robert Grudin writes: "Happiness may well be related to our attitude toward time."

Unhappiness, by extrapolation, may well be related to our inability to conjure up a constructive attitude toward time. I think of Malaysians I've met in my travels who claim they can stretch their "rubber time" to fit their needs rather than complain about not having enough it. Years ago, I went to a Golden State Warriors basketball game with swimmer Matt Biondi, winner of nine Olympic gold medals. That night, Charles Barkley scored fifty-six points, playing as if in super-slow-motion, I remarked in awe and wonder. Biondi nodded, saying it was no illusion, and that the great athletes live for those moments. When pressed, Matt admitted that, for him, time seemed to slow down as he swam faster.

What has become clear to me over the years is that people who are creative in any field use their time differently, whether manically or ingeniously, but generally more efficiently. Your effort in any endeavor is intimately connected to your attitude toward time. The way you handle the pressure of deadlines, money problems, health issues, and all the ordinary obstacles that *con*spire to keep you from being *in*spired determines how effective you will be when you sit down to write or paint or compose. Time travel is no mere sci-fi conceit for creative people. It's a way of life that treats the imagination as a time machine so you can live in the past, present, and future—at will.

What does all this tell us? There is no life of art without an art of time. Your art relies on your philosophy and practice of timing, which is why the second stage on the creative journey is to harness time itself. Rather than capitulating to the devilish habit of *killing* time, if you care about your imaginative powers, you must forge a new habit of *creating* time where there was none before. That means choosing carefully what you do and when you do it, with whom you spend your time, and whether you use your days making art or making excuses.

Sooner or later, you discover, as Annie Dillard puts it in *The Writing Life,* "The way we spend our days is the way we spend our lives." You learn the joy of knowing that art *doubles* life, allows you to relive, often at an even greater depth, experiences you didn't quite fathom the first time around.

EXERCISE 4: Five Excellent Ways to Seize the Moment

Stretch it. Don't be a time-victim. Think of your time as elastic. Stretch it for things that need to be done or enjoyed and eliminate the trivial and the frivolous.

Steal it. Think of Oliver Nelson's jazz album *Stolen Moments* and what the title implies. Rise an hour earlier for a week, go to bed an hour later for a

Nautilus shell on a farmhouse wall, Perigueux, France. Photograph by Phil Cousineau, 1985.

month. Make something out of it. Use the gift of extra time for your art.

Save it. Every time you have a numinous encounter with someone or something—a book, a painting, a movie, a building, any experience that moves you—*re-create* it for yourself. Write about it, commit it to canvas, photograph it if it was a blazing moment for you, like the startling sight for me of an ancient nautilus shell embedded in the wall of an old French farmhouse.

Slow down. Thoreau's famous maxim is more relevant than ever: "When in doubt, slow down." This is the American version of the old Italian art of *far niente,* doing nothing, but doing it alertly. The practice will renew you by reducing anxiety.

Swiftly, grab him. The old Greek saying about Kairos is still good advice: sacred time is quicksilver; seize it or lose it. Contrast it with ordinary time when we endure the inevitable grunt work; this will teach you the value of time.

No one can really teach you how to use your time better except through example, which is why grandparents are revered throughout the world and artists are both respected and reviled. You just have to look at everything that comes your way as an opportunity to learn.

Consider Henry Darger, a Chicago janitor by day and a visionary painter and cosmic novelist by night. In hermetic secrecy, he painted wild mythological worlds about a lost race on canvases twenty feet long, and used these to illustrate his 3500-page leather-bound novel. Darger was committed to an insane asylum at age 67. Shortly after, his only friend found his amazing work in his apartment. When the astounded friend inquired why Darger hadn't shared the work earlier, he sighed: "Too late now." Was it? Entire doctoral dissertations have been written on his compulsive secrecy and the mysterious drive behind his work, part of which is now in a permanent collection at the Art Institute of Chicago. Those three words haunt and taunt . . . to late for *what?*

MAXIMS TO LIVE BY

Be quick, but don't hurry. (Coach John Wooden)

You mean, now? (Yogi Berra's response to pitcher Tom Seaver's question, "What time is it?")

Ars longa, vita brevis. (Précis of an ancient maxim: "Life is short, art long, opportunity fleeting, experience treacherous, judgment difficult.")

This will be the week that was. (Grandma Dora to me, at ten)

Procrastination is the thief of time.

TIME ON FIRE

Have you ever suspected that time can catch fire? That we can burn daylight, kindle the darkness? You're not alone. Swiss psychologist Marie-Louise von Franz wrote: "The idea that time consists of dynamic and rhythmically structured patterns can be illustrated by the symbol of the old Chinese fire clock. This type of clock was constructed by spreading a combustible powder over a labyrinth and igniting it at one end, so that its burning head crept slowly forward like a fuse. Time was marked off according to the progress of the fire."

In other words, time burns, disappears, turns to ashes in our hands and hearts. To have more time, we have to *make time,* as counterintuitive as that may sound. In a car or a train, you can "make time" by going faster; but in your creative space, your studio, you "make time" by slowing down and stretching it. Or else you become a time-victim—a master procrastinator. You make sacred time by renewing yourself with solitude. The roots of genius are there, in the privacy of your own creative space, trying their best to spur your own unconscious impulses.

Of course, the classic example is composer Wolfgang Mozart, who wrote in a letter about the flares of inspiration that often forced him to stop his carriage in full flight and jot down whole symphonies. "When I am . . . completely myself, entirely alone or during the night when I cannot sleep, it is on such occasions that my ideas flow best and most abundantly. Whence and how these come I know not nor can I force them . . . Nor do I hear in my imagination the parts successively, but I hear them *gleich alles zusammen* (all at the same time all together)."

Each creative spirit has a different way of "making time." Poet William Stafford was forced to rise before dawn every day after his children were born to have a solid hour of privacy and silence in which to write. Georgia O'Keeffe hopped into her old woodie station wagon whenever she felt the well of inspiration run dry and drove out into the remote mountains, where she collected cow skulls, arrow heads, and sunsets. May Sarton fled the big city to live alone for a year in the New Hampshire countryside, because, as she wrote in *Journal of a Solitude,* she wanted to "take up my 'real life' again at last." Herman Hesse spent time in his garden to "free his mind" from work, saying later that much of his classic book *The Glass Bead Game* was composed while he relaxed there. Isabelle Allende sets a deadline for beginning each new book—January 8— that honors her memory of the day she began a five-hundred page letter to her dying grandfather, which became *The House of Spirits.*

As you think about ways that you can "make" creative time in your own life, consider these five questions:

What is your time *for?*

What can you do in the time allotted to you?

What are you doing when you aren't doing anything?

Do you believe you can make up for lost time?

If you steal time, do you ever have to give it back?

TIME AND THE ART OF LIVING CREATIVELY

When I look back over those critical times when I deliberately seized the day, I am amazed at the difference they made in my life. Once, while staying at the Old Ground Hotel, in Ennis, Ireland, I was overwhelmed with a sudden surge of confidence and determination. On some subconscious level, I knew I was facing a new opportunity. I grabbed a postcard from the hotel desk and, in less than five minutes, wrote to Stuart Brown, with whom I was collaborating on *The Hero's Journey*. Boldly, I volunteered to look over his book manuscript, knowing it had languished for four years. Two months later, Stuart asked me to take over and I had my first book contract.

Where does this sense of confidence come from, if not from an uncanny sense of destiny, a hint of what we're supposed to be doing with our lives? It is a constant source of consolation to me that I'm not alone in my compulsion to seize opportunity when it arises. I love reading how Leonardo da Vinci conscientiously reviewed his life on a daily basis. "It is of no small benefit on finding oneself in bed in the dark," he wrote in the notebooks, "to go over again in the imagination the main outlines of forms previously studied, or of other note-worthy things conceived by ingenious speculation."

To live time more fully, you must slow it down, which is one of the glories of the arts. Time is a sacred playground. With it—or without the wise use of it—there is no creativity. There is no good life without taking time for paradise, the walled garden beyond time. Auguste Rodin sculpted to get his hands around the tumult of time. Rilke wrote poetry to change his life. Calvino said he loved most those works that had a way of making time go backward. J. M. W. Turner tied himself to the masts of ships so he might feel the movement of time and taste the colors of the sea. The examples are endless and endlessly inspiring.

The clock is always ticking. Inspiration always fades. If you are most yourself when you are creating, where will you find the time to do what you are meant to do? How will you summon the courage to begin? Can creativity occur without a deliberate use of time? Is cultivating time and the art of creativity the first step toward an art of living? Are you beginning to glimpse the secret, or at least the mystery, of this thing called creativity? It's important, because your image of time determines the intensity of your focus and the heat of your desire to be creative.

When the New Zealand short-story writer Katherine Mansfield was forty years old, she spent an extended period in a health spa trying to cure her tuberculosis. On October 10, 1922, she addressed herself in her diary: "Now, Katherine, what do you mean by health?" She answered:

> By health I mean the power to live a full, adult, living, breathing life in close contact with what I love—the earth and the wonders thereof—the sea—the sun . . . Then I want to work. At what? I want to live so that I work with my hands and my feeling and my brain. I want a garden, a small house, grass, animals, books, pictures, music. And out of this, the expression of this, I want to be writing . . . . But warm, eager, living life—to be rooted in life—to learn, to desire to know, to feel, to think, to act. That is what I want. And nothing less. This is what I must try for."

Rockfish, Hopkins Reef/Monterey Bay. Photograph by Chuck Davis, 2005.

In his ambrosial book *Zen in the Art of Writing,* Ray Bradbury answers the pestering questions he gets about the origin of his ideas emphasizing the daily need to move forward. "Every morning I jump out of bed and step on a landmine. The landmine is me. After the explosion, I spend the rest of the day putting the pieces back together." He does this in a surprisingly simple fashion, by venturing into his museum-like writing studio and fingering one of thousands of travel souvenirs, or opening a dictionary and choosing a single word. He then seizes the memory, emotion, or word and, as Klee said, takes it out for a walk—which invariably results in a story he didn't even know he had in him. The operative word, again, is *seize,* as in the moment, our destiny as creative souls.

EXERCISE 5. Five Simple Ways to Make Time

Memorize great poems. Learn "Ozymandias," by Percy Shelley, or a Neruda love poem, or a Mary Oliver nature piece. Learning something by heart stretches time.

Keep the Sabbath. No one is ever going to knock on your door and award you an extra hour, day, or week. So devote one day a week to your spiritual life, which will, in turn, revitalize your mind, your body, and your artmaking.

Preserve something. Think of Grandma Moses' paintings of rural America, the otherworldly photographs of underwater kelp forests by Chuck Davis, O. Winston Link's photographs of the disappearing steam trains of Virginia. Every word, paint stroke, or photo halts the march of time so others can ponder *our* time.

Turn distractions into free time. Learn to say "no" to people who enervate you or events that exhaust you. Luxuriate in all the time freed up for your real work.

Remember Pudd'nhead Wilson's advice: Every day do two things you've been avoiding. Begin now.

The mythic thread described by Stafford is different for everyone, but I believe it provides us with an image for what is constant and continuous in your life, what connects you to the deepest purpose and meaning of your soul. Don't ever let go of the thread. The thread is the link, the connection, the continuity of your life. You can't stop time, but you can hold onto the thread that ties together your past, present, and future. Perhaps that's why the gesture in American Sign Language for "soul" is exactly that, the hand movement of pulling a thread out of the belly. The thread may be inspiration, love, desperation, or passion. But it's always, as psychologist Robert A. Johnson writes in his autobiography, "a slender thread," easily lost or severed, and imperative for us to hold onto.

EXERCISE 6. Solving the Mystery of Time

Find an old postcard. Write out or sketch a note to a teacher or coach from your youth. Tell that person who you are, who you've become. Ask what's happened to them.

Write a letter to a dead friend or relative. Say what you never said while they were alive.

Write a message to yourself, not to be opened until the next time you are taking time for granted.

Write a note *as if communicating on your death bed.* Who would you try to reach? What would you say with the precious time you have left?

Every day choose a way to practice the long view of life. "Read not the *Times,* read *Eternity,*" remarked Thoreau. Read an old book to balance the news; go star-gazing to balance the close-up work on your computer. Startle yourself.

Box Noetica, assemblage
by Maggie Oman
Shannon, 2005.

Reverie is the foundation for the creative spirit and reverence for time is the building block. The only solution to the problem of finding time for creative work is to make it—make time to make art. You will always be able to find a reason not to; the frightening thing is that we all have our own reasons. When you try to do everything, you do nothing very well. But as Gertrude Stein has proved, doing a little every day (thirty minutes) can produce a great body of work. Commitment is the key. If you commit yourself to it, you can produce a masterpiece every day. Creative people create by doing more with less time. They take back time that was snatched away and stretch it out to eternity, which is why honest, truthful, and bold, original work feels timeless. That's where creative works come from—recaptured time. That's why the creators of timeless works often shrug and claim they don't know how it all happened.

When you do your work for the love of it, for the joy of it, and let go of the need to understand the *why* of it, you complete the second stage of the creative journey and are ready to move on to the third—seeking guidance. What are you waiting for? There is no time to lose. Go in search of lost time, like Proust, Cezanne, and Mahler; celebrate your ability to time-travel, back and forth from your distant past to the voice of the future.

SEIZING THE MOMENT IN A NUTSHELL

Every hour is a god, every day divine.
Don't be a time-victim by claiming you don't
have any.
Make time for timely things in your life.

WHAT TIME IS IT ON THE JOURNEY?

Can you feel time slowing down
or speeding up as you work?

Will you ever find time to rekindle your fire?

Dancer in Bliss. Jean Erdman Campbell in performance, circa 1945. Photograph by Harold Swann. Courtesy of Jean Erdman Campbell.

CHAPTER 4

Seeking Guidance

O, muse, make this tale live for us in all its many meanings.

—Homer, *Iliad*

Many is the time I've been told that the single most useful advice I've given over the last twenty-five years is simply to read (or view) biographies, read (or view) biographies or autobiographies, such as Richard Ellman's study of W. B. Yeats, Reeder's study of Akhmatova, Leonardo's notebooks, Van Gogh's letters, Georgia O'Keeffe's memoirs, or films about the art spirit like *My Brilliant Career, Immortal Beloved,* and *The Horse's Mouth,* with Alec Guinness playing an eccentric genius painter. But augment these, I've long suggested, with parables about the mysterious way the creative fire connects us all. Here's one of my favorites:

A long time ago, the great Rabbi Baal Shem Tov saw catastrophe looming for his people. So he followed the ancient custom of the holy men of untold generations before him. He left the village where he lived and journeyed deep into the dark and dangerous forest. There, he lifted up his heart to God, lit a fire, and prayed. His words flared. A miracle occurred. His people were saved.

Years later, misfortune again threatened. Baal Shem Tov's disciple, Magid of Mezritch, heard the call to intercede with heaven and traveled deep into the forest. Once there, he was enshrouded with darkness and fear struck deep, like a sharp blade, in his heart. "Master of the Universe, listen to me," he cried. "I don't know how to light the fire, but I do know how to say the prayer." God listened and knew Magid's heart was righteous. Again, a miracle happened and the people were saved.

Time passed. The world turned. Chaos struck again. This time Magid's disciple, Rabbi Moshe Leib of Sasov, knew he must try to save his people. He followed the path deep into the forest and fell to his knees, humbled by a sudden realization. "Lord, I don't know how to light the fire. I've forgotten the prayer, but I do know this holy place in your sacred wood. This must be sufficient." God heard him and agreed. Miraculously, the people were saved once more.

More time passed. Again, disaster loomed.
Sitting at home in an old bent chair, Rabbi Israel
of Rizhyn knew in his heart what he had to do to
overcome terrible times. He held his head in his
hands and whispered. "I regret I'm unable to light
the fire. I'm sorry I don't know the prayer. I feel a
terrible sorrow that I can't even find the path left
by the elders for me in the forest. All I can do is tell
the story and I pray that this will be enough."

And it was enough. The old ones say God
loves people because he loves a good story.

What I love about this inexhaustibly rich tale is how it echoes the ancient belief that the world is held together by our stories. My close friend and film partner, the late Gary Rhine, in the traditional Jewish sense of *tikkun,* believed the heart of the world was broken, but that it could be healed through storytelling. He reassured me that it is through stories that we discover the key to our connection to the divine, to ourselves, to our tribe, our community. Nothing makes sense until you tell a story about it. Nothing saves your soul and your connection to your own past more than keeping the flame alive by telling stories about it. Nothing *means* until it's told in a story.

In his epic ballad, "Hallelujah," Canadian poet and singer Leonard Cohen describes the "secret chord" that David, "the baffled king," played on his lyre for God. What Cohen delivers in five glorious stanzas is a description of the need and the power to praise, even if life is, elliptically, a "cold and broken hallelujah." It is the act that saves us—the singing, the praising, the creating. This is how we rekindle the fire in the forest. And it is why art is "our unique survival tool," as playwright David Mamet puts it. The mysterious power that artists, mystics, and teachers have tapped through the ages is the power to deliver the healing stories and images. Memory may be sacred, but it's forever fading, like disintegrating filmstrips. Sometimes it disappears altogether because, as the Irish say, memory is a merciful editor.

Reverie, your source of imaginative power, also fades. The seized day turns to night and, the next morning, the inspiration is gone. What gladdens the heart one day saddens it the next—usually when you're faced with the reality of the sudden plunge of the journey into the depths of your soul.

So here you are, trying to move forward. You've drifted down the river of reverie, seized the moment, maybe even begun the project that will someday define you. You were on fire and then the fire cooled. Something happened to quench it—the sting of self-doubt, lack of time, disinterested family, money problems, or the realization you chose the wrong project.

It's called *life at the crossroads*. At the crossroads, the "wannabes" are separated from the "gottabes"—the poseurs from the possessed. It is here that novels are dropped, recorded songs left unreleased, stones abandoned uncarved, paints stranded on the palette—all the victims of fear, exhaustion, or laziness. At the crossroads, many are called, but few boogie.

THE CROSSROADS OF CREATIVITY

At the crossroads of creativity, the artist is like a pilgrim on the road to Assisi, greeted by local peasants whispering "Don't give up, don't give up." At the crossroads, we learn of our need for the guidance and support of a mentor, a model, an elder—someone who can keep us on the path. Emerson urged on the young Whitman; Louis Leakey believed in Jane Goodall when no one else did; Woody Guthrie encouraged Bob Dylan, even as he lay dying in a hospital. Despite our living in a more-ironic-than-thou era, we can still find mentors and muses, these sources of fiery encouragement, if we just look carefully enough and have the sense to accept their help when we find them.

What will you do? Who will you listen to? How badly do you want to move on? Maybe the gods will overlook you, but the great teachers tell us we have to look out for ourselves. At this critical juncture in your creative journey, you must be ready and willing to ask for help to get you past the crossroads and keep you on the path. To do this, you need confidence, encouragement, and a model you trust enough to emulate.

If you are stuck, seek some mythic guidance. This is the moment for the mentor, the muse, the wise elder. Your guide—whether found in the present or the past, in your studio or in an old book—can help you avoid calamity, encourage you, give you back your own heart, and, in some mysterious way, keep you going. Your guiding force may be as near to you as the vein throbbing in your neck. Everyone has what Ray Bradbury calls "a secret self"—a mysterious stranger who lives in the imagination and is responsible for creativity—who keeps them on the path and helps them through the journey. "You have to believe in [your] secret self—or you shouldn't be writing," he said in a provocative interview. When I was working for the seventh long year on *Deadlines,* my book of famous last words, I was a hair's breadth away from quitting. Then I came across an old book of wisdom from the desert fathers. I flipped it open at random and the first page I saw spoke to my very soul: "The legendary Father Tarphon, one of the immortal Wisdom Fathers, who spent his life in the desert, said, 'You are not required to complete the work; but neither are you free to desist from it.'" I carried on. I finished instead of flinching. Sixteen years later, the book is still being used in death-and-dying classes, hospices, and writing classes. You can't be sure where the thread is going to lead, but you can be sure you have to follow it.

"God—give me guts!" shouted the message on the locker room bulletin board. An extraordinary effort is required to achieve the prodigious creative works of this world. It takes an inordinate amount of energy and commitment to get past the crossroads and journey on to creativity. Because of this, many travelers on the creative path eventually quit, or turn in work that isn't quite their own or isn't the best they are capable of. Dorothea Brande, the short-story writer and author of *Becoming a Writer,* a classic study of the creative life, summed it up like this: "Succeed—or stop!" Her not so subtle message was that, if you keep going, if you pass the crossroads, you can journey farther and go deeper than you've ever gone before. In doing so, you can even "disturb the universe" and tickle the curiosity of others. But to succeed in that way, you need guidance—the help or example of a mentor. As Pausanius said: "No man can live without counsel." As you consider who your models are in your own creative process, ask yourself these three questions:

Who do you turn to when you're stuck?

Is there a mentor network in your community?

Do your guides lead you forward or hold you back?

THE MENTOR'S MISSION

In spring 1986, I interviewed Jeremy Irons at the Cannes Film Festival about his role in Roland Joffé's *The Mission* for the *Hollywood Scriptwriter*. In the movie, Irons played the part of a Jesuit priest in the South African rainforest who is caught in the crossfire between Italy, Spain, and Portugal as they struggled to carve up the New World.

"How did you prepare for such a grueling role?" I asked, curious as to how he came to know the character of the brooding priest.

"Actually," he replied, "I listened to his soul."

"And what did his soul tell you?" I asked, surprised.

"That we were closer than I anticipated," Irons answered, his eyes transfixed on mine. "We share a sense of moral torment and rebellion." He laughed.

Referring to Robert Bresson's famous statement that "There must be at a certain moment, a transformation, or there is no art," I asked him "What was yours?"

"I was raised in a family of atheists back in England. I'm not normally considered a religious man. Actually, I spent five weeks traveling through South America with a Jesuit priest named Daniel Berrigan. We would sit for hours, Daniel and I, picking each other's brains. He would ask me about acting techniques, and I'd ask him about ecclesiastical knowledge, the spiritual life. I virtually went into retreat with him in the rainforest. I learned that he was very similar to the Father Gabriel character I was supposed to play in the movie . . . But that's part of the mystery, isn't it, the wonderful journey of getting to know another human being. That's what happened as I learned the soul of my character."

As Irons rose to leave, he turned to me with what Berrigan later described as eyes "blazing like a fire when a handful of spice is tossed in," and said: "There's so little real mystery left anymore, except for the mystery of getting to deeply know other people, other cultures. That's what acting's all about. That's our *real* mission."

Twenty years later, rereading the transcripts of the interview, I'm still struck by the hush of humility and the 1000-yard stare that came over Irons when I asked him how he prepared for the part of the doomed priest. It was as if he'd started his career over with the film and needed to seek out an elder. Daniel Berrigan became that elder. The role of the priest could have been intimidating, daunting, but he rose to the challenge, passed the crossroads, and turned in one of the greatest performances of his career.

This trait of insatiable curiosity is one I've encountered in talented people in every field of creativity I've explored over the years. The willingness to learn, to be curious, and always to be humble enough to seek out teachers is apparent in everyone who *grows* in their work. The conscious decision to seek out wise counsel—to find your secret self—is the antidote for the persistent fear that inspiration can be extinguished at any moment. At a profound level, we know that we have to feed the fire constantly. We can do that by communicating with our secret selves and listening to the stories of our elders. "In everyone's life," Albert Schweitzer wrote, "at some time, our inner fire goes out. It can then burst into flame again by an encounter with another human being. We can all be thankful for those people who rekindle the human spirit."

What I learned from Jeremy Irons is that, no matter whether you are a beginner or a veteran, an unknown or a star, you will eventually reach a crossroads that you can't navigate alone. The crossroads marks the edge of the unknown—No Man's Land, Middle Earth, Lilliput, The Back of Beyond. There is a kind of barbed wire to warn those without a stout heart. It's no place for the feckless or fearful. What the great biographies and parables teach us is that there are great souls everywhere whose stories can help us through. If you reach out, in humility and sometimes humor, to those who've gone before, you too will keep going. The *constantly creative* seek counsel and advice, or at least solace and encouragement, from the stories of their elders. They believe what the Roman Plautus wrote 2000 years ago, "No man is wise enough by himself." In Stephanie Bennett's documentary film, *Joni Mitchell: Woman of Heart and Mind,* the Canadian singer and painter credits Bob Dylan with giving her the courage to write more personally. "Dylan opened the door for the rest of us to write directly to the listener." Singer-songwriter R. B. Morris agrees: "In a broad sense every western songwriter has been influenced by him, as every playwright has been influenced by Shakespeare. We live in the era of Dylan." Morris points out, however, that Dylan's greatest gift was "his commitment to create under whatever circumstances life throws at you."

Mentors are the characters in your own life-story who appear at the right place at the right time to get you back on track, redirect your attention, ignite your imagination, and ensure you've lit the right fire. They are personifications of your initiation into the mysteries. But then *you* must go to work.

GUIDING WORDS TO LIVE BY

The mentor's job is to show up and tell the truth;

The elder's job is to be present;

The rabbi's job is to pass the salt.

—*from one of my myriad café napkin notes.*

Mentors nudge you along to where you ought to be and guide you through the crossroads. Sometimes, this guidance comes in the form of harsh discipline; sometimes, it comes silently. Sometimes, the advice will make your spirits soar, as singer Nick Cave says his mind took flight the first time he came across a book of Leonard Cohen's poetry. Sometimes, you may shrink from it out of intimidation or fear, as Diego Rivera described in his *Memoirs* falling ill after seeing Velázquez' paintings in Madrid. For the prodigious and prolific novelist Thomas Wolfe, the creative process began in a whirling vortex and continued as pages flew off his pen and filled whole trunks that his famed editor, Max Perkins, then had to decode and decompress into books. Wolfe wrote:

> It was creative chaos and that proceeded slowly
> at the expense of infinite confusion, toil, and

error toward clarification and the articulation of an ordered and formal structure. My editor, who worked and strove and suffered with me through the greater part of this period, shrewdly and humorously likened the making of these books to the creation of the world as described in Genesis.

For Van Morrison, his mentors spoke through the Voice of America while he was growing up in Belfast in the persons of Ray Charles, Muddy Waters, Hank Williams, Leadbelly, the Carter Family, and Blind Lemon Jefferson. Listen closely and you can still hear their bluesy *aarrgghh* in his voice.

Early on, we sing along with our favorite singers, copy famous drawings, and write like our favorite authors to help us learn our skills. Some never get past this apprentice stage; others find their own voice and forge their own style. Witness Rembrandt after years of painting like Rubens, or Ray Charles after a decade of sounding like Nat King Cole, Lynda Barry after trying in vain to draw like R. Crumb.

Growing up in Detroit in the fifties and sixties, I was an ardent admirer of Ty Cobb. Cobb wrote and reveled in his autobiography, in which he talked about the old-timey days of "pancake gloves, washboard fields, cramped upper berths on endless rides over poor roadbeds, the indignity of lugging our own luggage, four men to a tub in hotels." I learned an important lesson from Cobb's storytelling, one that has stuck with me throughout my own creative career. "When the Tigers arrived in a road-trip town," Cobb wrote, "I learned beforehand whether some of the old-time, retired stars of the game lived there . . . while the other ballplayers were crap-shooting and beer-drinking back at the hotel, I'd be with these old boys, picking their brains. They were tremendous storehouses of knowledge. Sitting at their feet, I got all sorts of tips and inspiration."

What those old codgers saw in Cobb was an elusive quality—a spiritual hunger to learn from a lived life, a desire to hear from someone who's been there and knows what it's like up ahead. I see this hunger everywhere I go. It quivers in people who feel alone in their art. It's a hunger for conversation, for soul guides, for someone to help us through the crossroads and continue on our journey. It's the longing for a spark to be ignited and recognized. I do what I can, whenever I can, to fan that flame.

Authentic mentors speak to us in the spirit of the word itself, which, in its original Greek, means "mind-maker." They help us find and make up our own minds. At their best, they are like the Zen master in the classic *Zen in the Art of Archery,* by Eugen Herrigel, who practiced the art of "teachless" teaching. He insisted that his students first learn proper breathing, then patience, then unselfconscious practice. "The shot will only go smoothly," the master said, "when it takes the archer himself by surprise." That has become my own standard for art: is it *startling?*

EXERCISE 7. Four Ways to Reflect on Mentors

Identify winners. List the winners of the Academy Award for best supporting actor, best producer, best cinematographer, at the 1990 Oscars. Or any award ceremony longer than three years ago. How much does their success truly influence your work? What do they teach you about success?

Pay tribute to your real teachers. Father Gary Young, of Nazareth, Kentucky, recalls a schoolboy assignment from his English teacher, Sr. Mary Herbert, who instructed him to write a story about a picture he'd brought to class. "Many times, I'm reluctant," he says, "to discard a picture because a story is in it. I feel I have a 'responsibility to reveal it.'" Years later, he created an album in her honor of photo-stories, which he describes as helping him "cross the frontier of creativity."

Recall encouragement. Now think back to the first teacher who ever drew you aside and said, *"Excellent! Have you ever thought of becoming a writer, an artist, an architect, a set designer?"* Can you *feel* in your bones the difference between ephemeral glory and infinite influence? A celebrity and a soul guide? Someone who has truly recognized and sparked your talent?

Contact your mentors. Recall all those who first recognized the spark in you and saw what makes you unique. Now contact them. Show some gratitude. Can you hear their *aarrgghh* in your work? What about them lives on in you?

The Nine Muses. **Medieval engraving.**

THE MUSES' GIFT

Mentors, invisible or visible, guide our minds and our bodies. But there is another archetypal guiding force for those embarking on a creative journey that is found in museums all over the world. If you're feeling desolate, alone, abandoned, uninspired in your work, think about the role the muses play in your life.

In her book *The Nine Muses,* anthropologist Angeles Arrien traces the word muse back to the Greek verb *muein,* "one who initiates somebody into the mysteries." They are, she writes, "creative messengers . . . they are often referred to as sacred epiphanies . . . they ignite our creativity, inspire our soul, invite us to be resourceful." The ancients portrayed them as nine women—the daughters of Memory who beckon us down the road of creativity. They are personifications of the forces of nature, symbols of the divine forces, and guides in the making of things. Contemplation of the muses can take you back to the looted library of memory, personal and cultural, to the deepest recesses of your recollective powers out of which all creativity comes.

The nine muses embody the urge to create in all its fiery forms. First and foremost, to remember (Mnemosyne), then to read or compose epics (Calliope), to study history (Clio), to love poetry (Erato), to study music (Euterpe), to plunge into the sorrows of the world (Melpomene), to use your gift of oratory (Polyhymnia), to dance (Terpsichore), to laugh (Thalia), and to gaze at the night sky (Urania). Their power is rooted in the fundamental magic of mimesis. They *motivate* us to create—which is to say, they *move* us to *make* something.

"[The muse] first makes man inspired," writes Plato in the *Ion,* "and then through these inspired ones others share in the enthusiasm, and a chain is formed, for the epic poets, all the good ones, have their excellence [arete], not from art, but are inspired, possessed, and thus they utter all these admirable poems."

If you want to learn about creative people, ask them who their muses are, who has moved or inspired them. Architect David Mayernik told me, in an interview for the documentary film *City 21,* that he uses history (Clio) to move his students, believing that it's impossible to teach ineffable concepts like "beauty" and "cultural memory" to students who've never encountered it. Mayernik takes his students "on a journey into the wonder and beauty of the Italian mind" in an effort to help them see they can use the past to revitalize our modern cities. Another architect, Anthony Lawlor, described to me recently how he invigorates his own work: "I go to a museum and sit in front of a painting and write a dialogue with the artist. The practice has unearthed some amazing insights. Sitting in front of a Monet haystack and asking him about his creative process produced some memorable exchanges that have helped me in my work to this day. I started doing this spontaneously when I was five. The first time was with Picasso's *Child Holding a Dove* and I slipped into the spirit of the child in the painting and Picasso's own spirit. I sensed a link to a kindred soul and that moment opened me up to the world of inspired art."

The muse personifies the upsurge of the life force so vital for creativity. But, as Plato reminds us, you flirt with danger if you're vainglorious enough to try to create without her, or if you believe that technical virtuosity is enough to win the day. "He who approaches the Temple of the Muses without inspiration," Plato writes, "in the belief that craftsmanship alone suffices, will remain a bungler and his presumptuous poetry will be obscured by the songs of the maniacs."

For me, this image of the chain of influence rings true. I think of the people who moved me to create: my Aunt Barb who gave me my first camera, my college journalism teacher who encouraged me to become a journalist, my college girlfriend

Venus de Milo on Santorini, Greece. **Photograph by Phil Cousineau, 2005.**

who urged me to follow my dream to travel around the world, and the dancer-choreographer Jean Erdman, who has inspired me by embodying the muses' message of inspiring others through grace and beauty. They are all part of the chain of my own creativity. But not all muses are alive, at least physically. Some live on in books, music, dance, or theater. My own discovery of Sappho while traveling through the Greek islands was a revelation for me, and became another link in my chain of influences.

Who has acted as a muse in your life, and who might do so now? Who has personified grace and beauty for you? Who has inspired in you a dedication to excellence and virtue? Who has warned you about hubris? The following exercise describes valid ways to invoke your own muse. Pick one to start with. If it doesn't relate to you and your creative work, choose another. Come back to them over and over.

EXERCISE 8. Nine Ways to Invoke the Muses

Remember to remember (Mnemosyne). This was Tolstoy's last great piece of advice, but also an echo of the sublime Greek insight that memory is the mother of the Muses. The more we recall them, the more they infuse our creative work. Make a 30-day practice of writing down ten things you want to remember each day. Lists are luminous, if seen as numinous. Memory is a muscle that must be flexed every day.

Read and study history (Clio). Recall Seneca's prescient words, that those who don't know where they came from remain children. But history isn't only instructive; it's humbling. Read a biography or novel about one of your creative people from times past, and then fictionalize the story in a way that makes it relevant for today.

Memorize love poetry (Erato). When in doubt, learn it by heart. The gorgeous love poems of Sappho, Neruda, Kinnell, and Olds never fail to light the candle in the heart.

Start singing (Euterpe). Angeles Arrien recommends that those who are stuck in their work start belting out their favorite song. The breathing and emotion involved in singing stirs the smoldering embers. Sing a song out loud. If you've never sung before, learn a new song and sing it in the shower. Tell your neighbor Sinatra said it's good for the soul.

See a war movie (Melpomene). Take Socrates' advice to "practice dying" and, like Melpomene, plunge into the sorrows of the world. To know is better than not to know; to know the rapacious reality of war can make you appreciate every day far more. Follow the accounts of a current conflict. Then reexamine your current work: does it have the requisite "dark thread" that reflects the shadow of the times?

Speak up (Polyhymnia). I once asked the American Indian writer Vine DeLoria, Jr. what he recommended to help his people revive their culture. "Revive oratory," he said in a heartbeat. You don't know what you think until you've had to declare what you stand for. Give an impassioned speach. You have a private voice, but have you found your *public* voice?

Go dancing (Terpsichore). In the terpsichorean tradition, dance your truth, get grounded. Patronize and support a local dance troupe—attend performances, help build sets, make costumes. Make your words dance on the page, your lines caper across the canvas.

Lighten up (Thalia). Leaven your next business meeting with some jokes; focus on the light side. Remember why angels can fly—they take themselves lightly.

Gaze at the night sky (Urania). This is a time-honored tradition for learning the long view. Go a step further, like the father in the Ethan Canin short story—make up a few constellations. Name them. It ensouls the night sky and provides a literally cosmic perspective for our microdramas here on earth.

The nine muses and innumerable mentors who are available to us remind us again and again that we need not go it alone on the creative journey. They will inspire and guide, but they will not, they cannot, do the work for us. We still need to strike the flint, put pen to paper, brush to canvas, chisel to stone, fingers to the keys. They lure, but we must endure.

Finally, a word about muses and mentors in one small package. In 1978, I met an older woman in Ukiah, California, Enid Hilton. She had grown up in the north of England to

Enid Hilton, raconteur extraordinaire, Ukiah, California, 1978. Photograph by Phil Cousineau.

bohemian parents whose Sunday afternoon teas were legendary. On any given weekend the young Enid would sit down with the likes of Virginia Woolf, Isadora Duncan, Aldous Huxley, and her favorite, D. H. Lawrence.

"When I was in my preteens," she told me one afternoon at her home, "I told everyone I was going to be an artist. 'DHL' came by that afternoon and asked me what I was going to be when I grew up and I told him, a writer. Well, he asked to look at my work, and so I fetched it. When I showed it to him, he took it very seriously and with much energy and concern. Then with tact and care he said, 'I think, Enid, for the time being, I'd stick to painting.'"

Enid laughed and said it was the best advice she ever got. She went on to become an artist, teacher, political activist, and book smuggler. It was she who snuck into the U. S. the first three clandestine copies of *Lady Chatterley's Lover,* in thanks to Lawrence, who had helped shape her life. Her story celebrates the lanternlike power of mentors and muses, the power of inspiration that can be passed down from generation to generation in often unexpected ways.

Mentors and muses personify light and hope. They move us to create; they keep us on the path; they inspire us to succeed. French poet Guillaume Apollinaire captures this moment of divine collaboration perfectly in his poem "The Edge":

> *"Come to the edge," he said.*
> *They said, "We are afraid."*
> *"Come to the edge," he said.*
> *They came.*
> *He pushed them . . . and they flew.*

SEEKING GUIDANCE IN A NUTSHELL

> *Mentors help us make up our own mind and*
> *nudge us to make our own way.*
> *Muses inspire us, as Grandma used to say, nine*
> *ways from Sunday.*
> *Soul guides lead us back to our selves.*
> *Praise the bridge that carries you across.*

ARE YOU HUMBLE ENOUGH
TO ASK FOR HELP?

How many of the muses infuse your life?

Do you remember to remember
every day as if it were a sacred vow?

PART II

Perspiration

We work in the dark—we do what we can—
we give what we have—Our doubt is
our passion
and our passion is our task. The rest is the
madness of art.

—Henry James, *The Middle Years*

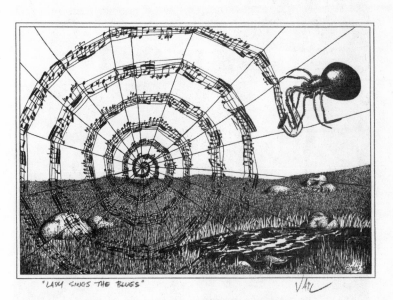

Lady Sings the Blues. Pen & ink by Stuart Vail Balcomb, 1984.

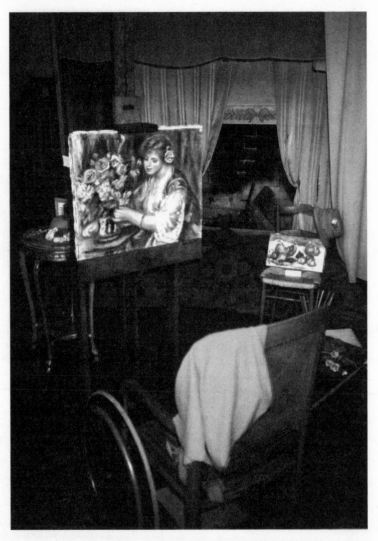

Renoir's Studio, Nice, France. Photograph by Phil Cousineau, 1997.

CHAPTER 5

Creative Space

The only thing you really need is the talent of the room.
Unless you have that, your other talents are worthless.

—Michael Ventura, "The Talent of the Room,"

While the initial stages of any creative process are infused with the three aspects of inspiration—reverie, time, and guidance—the second part of the journey requires action. After the journey down and back into your soul, where filmmaker Federico Fellini reminds us dwell both the treasure and the dragon, you must work toward the work itself. As physicist John Wheeler, famed for the discovery of black holes, writes: "Life is renewed from underneath."

There is a tension, however, between the work of creative genius and the work of the mundane—between inspiration and perspiration, between idea and deed, between vision and creation. It is here that so many falter. It is here that fear kicks in and paralysis overcomes your body, your mind, and sometimes your soul. So it's imperative that you think deeply about the difference between the *unreal* work you do in life and the *real* work—the soul work that is closer to vocation, the work that connects you to your ancestors, your land, your community. The distinction is palpable and merciless. Unreal work burns you out; real work renews you. Unreal work conspires to make you repeat yourself or copy others; real work gives you the courage to create your own unique style.

One of the great writers on the lapidary nature of labor, Eric Gill, said in *A Holy Tradition of Working,* "The imagination is the faculty by which what the eye sees and what the mind thinks about it is re-created into what the man loves." Seen in this way, creativity is an act of unique communication, evidence of your soul's move from inspiration to perspiration,

Joseph Campbell at his desk in Honolulu. Photograph by Phil Cousineau, 1985.

from the invocation "You must change your life" to the charge "You must create your life." Igor Stravinsky, in his classic book on music, *Poetics of Music in the Form of Six Lessons,* characterized this move as one that "helps us pass from the level of conception to the level of realization." As we've learned from countless commentators on the artistic temperament since Vasari, including Freud, Barthes, Dillard, and Becker, creative people encounter life as a problem that must be solved. The object or the performance is a fiery response to that problem pressing on your soul.

THE TALENT OF A ROOM

All creativity happens somewhere—in a study, in a studio, on a stage, in a garret. That space is where the creation comes to life, where the work actually happens—or doesn't. It's where the alchemy occurs—or flames out. It's where the spark is ignited—or extinguished. That's why artists' creative space— their rooms—have been mythologized over the centuries and why this space is essential to all our creative journeys. In his conversation with Bill Moyers in *The Power of Myth,* Joseph Campbell described the need for "a room . . . where you can simply experience what's coming forth from what you are and what you might be. This is the place of creative incubation." The creator of *Peanuts,* comic strip artist Charles Schultz once said, "Working in the same room gives you security; it turns on the creativity." Others need to move from room to room.

Over the last few decades I've lived in wondrous rooms—in Dublin, London, Paris, Manila, Lisbon, and now San Francisco. In every one of them, I can chronicle a leap forward or a stultifying grinding to a halt of all my dreams and best intentions. Beyond my own rooms, I've also tramped the world's back roads to visit the homes of dozens of writers, poets, artists, sculptors, filmmakers, musicians, painters, composers, scientists, and architects.

Often, I've gone alone, because my fellow travelers thought it beneath them—an activity that smacked of hero worship or superstition. I didn't care. I was after an encounter, evidence of a lived life, remnants of a story beyond the legends and myths of the artist's world I'd been raised to believe in. I've always loved the traces of a creative life left behind on desktops, easels, cameras, blueprints, or test tubes. Call it what you will—a presence, a residue, a physical record of something sacred, the release and transcendence of talent, a lingering persistence, an echo of something significant—it moves me. It makes palpable to me the alchemy of creativity. It makes the creative act deeply *real*.

One of my most moving experiences with the power of a creative space occurred in Russia. I went to visit Fountain House, the home of Anna Akhmatova, the poet of Mother Russia, known in cellars, salons, and cabarets from the Kremlin to Siberia. I found the museum guard, an old babushka named Fiona, sitting on a three-legged stool with the fabled writer's book at her side. When I asked if she'd ever met the poet, she beckoned me closer and, in the hushed tones of someone who'd lived in fear of the KGB all her life, told me the story of the ghostly rooms.

The mansion had been turned into "The House of Curious Science" after the carnage of the 1917 Revolution. When the museum ran out of funds, Akhmatova settled into the west wing, where she wrote requiems for fallen heroes and poems for lost lovers.

Akhmatova had a supernatural confidence in the abiding duty of writers to say the unsayable. Her courage inspired clandestine evenings in the smoke-curdled rooms, where she was besieged by admirers to recite her verse. Rather than risk the horrors of prison by committing her poems to paper, she committed them to memory and demanded that everyone who heard them learn them by heart, then, like old-world apostles, pass them on in a kind of literary telegraph system to others in the underground resistance movement. They, in turn, were obliged to memorize them and pass them on again.

As I turned to leave the poet's rooms, the wizened old guard leaned toward me to confide one last thing: "What we learn by heart learns about us."

If it isn't a Russian proverb, it should be.

Forty-five years after Akhmatova's death in 1962, literary pilgrims from all over the world make the haj to St. Petersburg to wander the dimly lit, foam-green rooms with their glass cases full of the poet's manuscripts, foreign editions, letters, glasses, pens, and papers. Stalin feared Akhamatova more than any other figure during his reign of terror because she reached down into her soul to express the inexpressible.

And it all came from a room.

And so it is that, after all the bowing to the altar of artistic mystery, we long to touch a writer's desk and understand what transpires in an artist's room—angelic whispers into all-too-human ears, hands that grasp real pens, heads that lean over real typewriters, shoulders that slump over real easels, fingers that race over real piano keys—all doing something impossible, something paradoxical.

The room is where creative people make something out of nothing. The room is where life comes to life. First, there was an empty mind, then an idea, then an artifact, then a real thing. That's what mesmerizes us about creative people. To outsiders, they seem like magicians; to insiders, they seem like worker bees. When we learn their stories, read their biographies, view their documentaries, or listen to the gossip, we get closer to the mystery. When we visit their homes, it's like looking up the sleeve of the magician. If we see the *where,* maybe we'll understand the *how.*

When you stand in the Paris studio of a prolific sculptor like Antoine Bourdelle, have coffee at the Lisbon café where Fernand Pessoa drank every day, or spend time in Gaudi's studio in Barcelona, you feel the pull of the numinous. But that tug isn't felt only in the glamorous rooms of the successful. It beckons from heartbreaking walls as well—from Auschwitz and Dachau, where prisoners played concertos on cardboard violins and the Man Who Offered Himself as a Library recited by heart from his prodigious memory. It beckons from the *oubliettes* beneath the streets of Paris, where prisoners etched there last words into the stone walls with their fingernails. It beckons from Geronimo's cell in Florida, where he wrote his heartbreaking memoirs.

What fascinates me in these rooms is the irrepressible urge to communicate *under any circumstances.* I hope to understand by standing where it happened. Returning to the source, the wellspring, the spot where creative waters gushed forth can have a miraculous effect. The Greeks called it *mimesis*, the astonishing ability of human beings to mimic behavior, and the principle remains as powerful today as it was then. Think about the power of a book—*Uncle Tom's Cabin*—or the power of a song—*If I Had a Hammer*—or the power of public architecture—the Vietnam War Memorial—and how they have galvanized tens of millions of people with their messages. They *moved* people, and people who are *moved, move* others, magically, from one room to another.

A ROOM OF YOUR OWN

Artists from Virginia Woolf to the Beach Boys have written and sung about everyone's need for a room of their own. When Annie Dillard interviewed Eudora Welty at her Mississippi home, Welty described her writing room as her "focusing point," where all her dreams came to life. Indeed, Pascal once said that all the world's problems could be linked to the inability of men to stay in their rooms.

What about you? Do you have a creative space that ignites your creative fires? Can you forge the creative solitude necessary to make art there?

Joyce Carol Oates describes her room like this: "I love my study. It's the place to which I return, with myriad daydreams, sketchy memories, scraps of paper." She recalls Emily Dickinson's habit of writing on scraps of paper, then folding them in her pockets and ruminating over them later in the day. Aha! Vindication! Now I don't feel quite so eccentric about unfolding my café napkins, matchbook covers, ticket stubs, tollbooth receipts, and beer coasters and trying to decipher them hours, days, months, years later. The ancients used to call this *silva rerum*, the "forest of things"—the myriad details that make up a life. These details can bring an artist's work to life for you far better than a career of speculating abstractly about their creative genius. Years of only reading and arguing about art can make you forget that artists are real people with real pulses, real dandruff, real debts—and that they are the ones who do the real work.

This piercing realization is enlightening. As Michael Ventura wrote in his essay that gives this chapter its epigraph, "The room, you see, is a dangerous place. Not in itself, but because *you're* dangerous . . . Every single word leads, in this way, to the same destination, your soul. Which is, in part, the soul of everyone. Every word has the capacity to start the journey. And once you're on it, there is no knowing what will happen." So all this vaunting of writing rooms, artist studios, and dance floors is potentially demoralizing. One visitor's epiphany is another visitor's paralysis. Unless, that is, you learn how to transfer that mythic power to your own creative space. Otherwise, the grandest of plans can devolve into exercises of often comic futility. Playwright Budd Schulberg humorously admitted as much: "First, I clean my typewriter. Then I go through my shelves and return all borrowed books. Then I play with my three children. Then, if it's warm, I go for a swim . . . By then it's time to clean my typewriter again."

EXERCISE 9. Four Ways to Create Your Own Room

Create a reverie environment. To create, you must time-travel. One of the many unauthorized biographies of Van Morrison tells the story of how often the great Irish bard/rock star goes back in his memory, drifts in reverie, to Belfast, where he grew up listening to Armed Forces Radio broadcasting rhythm-and-blues. That music, Morrison said, triggered his dream to become a singer. Create a space for yourself that triggers reverie and encourages you to imagine and dream. Amy tan uses furniture from Imperial China to evoke the right mood. Saul Bellow wrote standing up at a tilted architecture table. Edward Hopper installed large windows to stare out at the sea. Ray Bradbury left his writing room at home to write *Fahrenheit 451* in the basement of the UCLA library on a rented ten-cents-an-hour typewriter.

Set aside time for play. In *Wordplay*, the 2006 documentary about the cultural phenomenon of the *New York Times* crossword puzzle, ex-President Bill Clinton diffidently describes his habit of parallel thinking: "Sometimes you have to go at a problem like I'd go at a crossword," he says. "I rarely work a puzzle of any difficulty from end to end. I do it irrationally, illogically. A lot of difficult, complex problems are like that. You have to find some aspect you understand, then you unravel the mystery you're trying to understand. We're all capable of doing more than we think [we can]." Establish a space where your mind can travel down irrational and illogical paths. Follow those paths to new places and new ideas.

Cultivate enthusiasm in your room. Remember Emerson's immortal words: "Nothing great was ever accomplished without enthusiasm." One surefire way to create a space you'll always want to return to is to cultivate your passions—what Emerson describes as the power that fuels your creativity, which is just another way to say your divine inclinations, including your dreams and your epiphanies. Enthusiasm is the release of the god within, but it is also the spark for the gods without. So let go of the cool hunter inside you that keeps you from expressing your love, your passion, your enthusiasm for life. Go back to where it all began—let your soul move you back to the path of reverie and then slingshot you forward on the path to creativity.

Create your own Cabinet of Wonder. Many visitors enter my basement dream world and shout out something like: "It's a museum, not a studio!" I take this as a compliment, because my room is filled with souvenirs and mementos from all over the world. I merely have to swivel my head to travel from the Arctic to the tip of South America. It's here that I court my private passions, from baseball to photography. Make sure that your room is filled with those things that make you passionate, make you curious, make you alive, and more vital yet, make you want to *work*. Enthusiastically, not grudgingly.

In fall 2003, I visited Rembrandt's Amsterdam studio, a large room now fitted out with reproductions of his work and replicas of his painting tools and brushes. I had the great good fortune to arrive at the precise moment when the curator carefully opened a wall of ten-foot-high shutters, letting in a beautiful golden light that slowly bathed the room. In that privileged moment (as Proust would have it), I caught a glimpse into the secret of Rembrandt's famed chiaroscuro—that unique smoky-gold light that sets his art apart from that of any other artist. With that warm winter sun on my face, I experienced the miracle of Rembrandt's light and understood why he was compelled to paint through the agony of bankruptcy and public ridicule. I knew how a room could talk, could give the gift of courage, could compel an artist to create.

An Evening with Dr. Samuel Johnson at the Mitre Tavern, London.
Eighteenth-century engraving.

Many times over the years, I've consulted with students and professionals who were stuck at the beginning of a project, their engines idling, their souls at bay. One of my first questions in this situation is: "What is your work space like? Do you feel inspired in your writing room or studio? If not, why not?" A writer from Santa Cruz once told me she had no space of her own, she only wrote in her car, in supermarket parking lots, sometimes under streetlights. She'd written half a novel, but couldn't seem to finish it. First, I regaled her with stories of other famous artists who had worked in similar situations—Dr. Johnson, who used to write in taverns; J. K. Rowling, who wrote the first drafts of *Harry Potter* on a commuter train; John Mulligan, who wrote his memoirs when he was homeless and living on a bench in Washington Square Park; Michael Blake who wrote the screenplay for *Dances with Wolves* while living in his Volkswagon. Then, knowing that she had a little extra money each month, I suggested that she either convert some space in her basement or rent a cheap office to use just for her writing. Within a year, she'd completed her novel.

SACRED SPACE

The brilliant dancer and photographer Trish O'Reilly, who had worked with Mother Theresa, told me how every home in India, from hovel to palace, has an inviolate corner for prayer and meditation or art-making. From this, I learned an important truth: Sacred space is needed if sacred work is to be done. You must find a way to transform even the most mundane room into numinous atmosphere.

In this numinous sense, the room is more than a physical space; it is psychological, spiritual, and mythic—it houses the crossroads of creativity. Father John Dear, a Jesuit priest, peacemaker, and prolific author, found himself at a point in his life at which he knew he needed solitude and silence if he was to carry on with his work. He chose several weeks of silent retreat in Thomas Merton's hermitage on the grounds of the Abbey of Gethsemani near Louisville, Kentucky. "That sacred space changed, no, it *saved* my life," he told me, claiming he was "slowly transformed . . . lost in the moment, the sanctity of the place . . . My old self, my old shell, cracks and falls off . . . "

Architect Anthony Lawlor, who specializes in creating sacred spaces for people around the world, reflects on the power of those spaces: "When you enter the room each day, be conscious of crossing the threshold, sitting in your chair, how the materials you use to create support the act of creation. Pin the creation of each day on the wall so at the end of a week you have a visible collection of your creative efforts. Keep occupying this room every day and build on the work from the first seven days."

Do you have a sacred space in which to pursue your art? Have you designed a workspace that thrills you when you enter, a space you dream about at night and are eager to get back to the next day? Or do you dread going back to the computer, the design table, the potter's wheel? Use this simple exercise to help you create a reliable space for your creative work, a place to muse and perform the *real work*.

EXERCISE 10. Creating Sacred Space

Draw a floor map of the house you grew up in.

In your mind and with your pen, walk from room to room. What images and stories are still there?

Now draw a map of your current workspace. Is there any point of overlap? Recreate some detail.Now draw the floor plan of the house or apartment you now dwell in. Where is your creative space? Is it incidental or central to your life? Do others know it is sacred to you? If not, tell them. Be clear about it. Create a ritual that sanctifies this room. Personalize it by hanging family photo, travel mementos, icons from your craft that lend the room a sense of holy mystery.

Reorganize your space until it completely reflects your deepest creative intentions. Forget trendy; this is your *real* life you're trying to fathom. Give yourself permission to leave mundane chores behind. Forget the dishes, laundry, and yard work. Don't worry. They'll be there when you finished your artmaking for the day. Seal yourself off; secret yourself away. The rest can wait; your soulwork can't.

Poet, essayist, and children's book author Donald Hall describes the ideal writing room as one that encourages "absorbedness," a marvelous word that captures the mystery of that condition known as *flow* that comes from a life of devotion, discipline, and desire. San Francisco painter Gregg Chadwick agrees: "I need everything to be just right, the music, the food, the light, the way my books are aligned on my bookshelves, before I can start to paint. I need to be rigorous about my work because there's so much pressure just to create *product* that it's hard to create art unless I *feel* like an artist and not just a businessman when I'm painting."

Norwegian painter Laila Carlson underscored this point in an interview with me in late 2006. "When I am working I am being true to myself," she said, "even if no one ever sees or likes my work; when I'm not working I feel like I'm not myself. I'm somebody else and I'm miserable." You have to love your work; you have to have a longing to understand some deep mystery. When your environment is finally right, the work comes by itself. I get this same reaction from people who've found the secret to creative life—doing what they want to do, need to do. Grammy-award winning singer Joanne Shenandoah once told me that her ability to work depends upon the sanctity of the right room at the right time. "Most times," she reports, "my schedule is such that I *must* go to my studio because I rarely have the *time* to be creative . . . If I light my candles, burn my sage and sweet grass, all flows beautifully, even if I'm living through difficult times. When I'm in there I feel a small bit of calm, which allows me to write my songs." When you sequester yourself in this way, you can become yourself—you can meander into the cave of your soul and seize the treasure otherwise sealed away. You can escape into a fantasy in which your art can thrive. Going to your room can be like making a pilgrimage to the unlived life. "I am here alone for the first time in weeks," May Sarton wrote in *Journal of a Solitude,* her 1973 account of a year spent alone in a New Hampshire beach house. Her valiant attempt to plunge into "the rocky depths, to the matrix itself . . . the huge, empty silence" is a brave and inspiring one and has become symbolic to many of the soul time needed to complete important projects. "I have time to think," she says of her inward pilgrimage. "That is the great, the greatest luxury. I have time to be. Therefore my responsibility is huge."

So huge, in fact, it behooves you to prowl other rooms in search of inspiration — or vindication — of your insistence for the right atmosphere. Remember the wizened words of Alexandre Dumas, of *The Three Musketeers* fame, "To make a drama, a man needs passion and four walls."

Personally, the room that's most moved me was one of the simplest—Auguste Renoir's studio in the south of France. Nothing had been moved in the room since the day the great painter died in the 1930s. The wheelchair he died in was still a few inches away from the easel where he'd been working—the same chair to which he'd nailed himself in his later years so he wouldn't be tempted to move. An enlarged photograph of Renoir at work loomed nearby. In the photo, his hands are as

The Milwaukee poet Antler meditating in the room where Allen Ginsberg passed away in April 1997. Photograph by Jeff Poniewaz, 1998.

gnarled as the olive trees in the beautiful garden behind the house. The image recalled to me the artist's words in Vollard's marvelous book about him: "Oh, I don't mind the arthritis; it means I can't do anything but paint for the rest of my life." I read those words when I visited Renoir's studio in 1997. A few minutes later I stared out the window at a giant olive tree in his garden. The gnarled pattern in the bark was the mirror image of the artist's arthritic hands. Realizing what he endured to keep painting, I left with my hope restored for my work. The Milwaukee poet Antler had a similar experience when he visited the room in which Allen Ginsberg died. Knowing about Ginsberg's long agony and feeling his spirit in the room, Antler vowed to redouble his own determination to write as much as he can with his own remaining time.

CREATIVE SPACE IN A NUTSHELL

Where you create is where your heart is.
Reorganize your room regularly. Make your
room into a memory palace.

WHERE ARE YOU WHEN YOU'RE IN YOUR CREATIVE SPACE?

Can you harness the energies of your imagination there?

Have you found a place you can't wait to get to
in the morning and find it hard to leave at night?

Comanche Fancy Dancer, Cache, Oklahoma. Photograph
by Phil Cousineau, 1988.

CHAPTER 6

Deep Focus

> *You're involved in the action and vaguely aware of it— your*
> *focus is not on the commotion but on the opportunity ahead.*
> *I'd liken it to a sense of reverie . . . the insulated state a musi-*
> *cian achieves in a great performance . . . not just mechanical,*
> *not only spiritual; something of both, on a different plane and*
> *a more remote one.*
>
> —Arnold Palmer

We are all endowed with a certain fire at birth. Call it soul, spirit, talent, genius, initiative, or ambition. As you grow older, you decide whether or not to tend that fire. If you ignore it, something in you flames out; if you stoke it, stir it up, that something flourishes, though you may never know its secret identity or power. Physicist Sir Arthur Eddington said, after the discovery of black holes: "Something out there is doing we don't know what." So it is with the mysterious dark forces of creativity.

We're driven by hidden powers we barely understand. They compel us to write, draw, design, sing, sculpt, dance, or compose. That's why we often talk about ideas or inspirations "coming out of the blue" or being "channeled." Something *in there,* in us, is doing we don't know what. The trouble is that the state of euphoria that carries you like a raft on white water through the early stages of the creative journey doesn't last forever. Even if you're among the fortunate ones who learn how to cultivate your reveries, seize the moment and make time, connect with the soulful guidance of your muses, and commit to the talent of the room, you must descend further. More is required of you than the glint of an idea, no matter how clever it is. You have to pass the crossroads from wishful thinking to committed making—the doing of something over and over until it's right. As Leonard Cohen said in the film *I'm Your Man,* "If you want to be a writer, you have to go to work everyday." And to work effectively, you have to learn the art of deep concentration.

Those who aren't committed fall away. Those who believe that first drafts, first cuts, first thoughts are the stuff of creativity lose their way. Those who are easily distracted by the bombardment of pop culture, phone calls, emails, virtual worlds, or social responsibilities simply drift away. But those who go on go deeper and complete the journey. The $64,000 question is whether you can stay on the path long enough to finish what you started. The difference is the fire of your focus, the focus of your fire. "Drink fire on your journey!" shouted the drunk poet one rainy night in North Beach. "Life is a slow burn!"

"WHAT WILL IT TAKE FOR YOU TO MOVE?"

In 2002, when I was delivering one of my first "Creative Fires" lectures, one of the soundmen approached and asked if I had time for a story. Well, as you may suspect, I always have time for a story, so I smiled and nodded. He took me aside and spun this yarn:

An old mountain man refused to leave his mountain cabin to make way for a Tennessee Valley Authority project. After months of arguing, the project engineer finally asked in desperation: "What will it take for you to move, you old codger?"

"Y'all just don't get it, do ye?" the old man replied. "My grandfather lit this here fire over one hundred years ago," he said, pointing to the old stone fireplace. "My father kept it lit all his born days. I've kept it lit all mine. That there fire's never gone out. You wanna know why I ain't movin? 'Cuz that there fire . . . if it goes out, I goes out."

The engineer thought for a moment, then walked over to the backhoe operator waiting in the yard. A few minutes later, they began digging a trench under the cabin and lifted it lock, stock, and barrel onto the back of a waiting truck. The truck deposited its load—complete with flickering fire—in a new location out of the way of the dam project. The mountain man settled in and stoked his fire for many more years.

"That engineer was my father," the soundman added.

When he finished telling his story, the soundman turned to me and said: "You're on fire this morning, Phil. I'm not really sure what you're talking about, but I think the old mountain man was talking about the same thing."

What I think he meant was that my *creative* fire and the old mountain man's *ancestral* fire are linked by spirit. They both refer to the life force, the continuity of the generations, the connection to the land, and in some strange way, the fierce ability to *focus* on what matters most. And yet to use the words focus and fire in the same sentence is almost tautological.

After all, it's no accident—unless a happy accident of serendipity—that "focus" is the Latin word for fireplace—which leads to an image that delights me. The ability to focus—to concentrate, look deeply, bring your attention to a point—comes from thousands of years of sitting contemplatively around campfires, hearths, candles, and torches. With this powerful image come echoes of vision, heat, light, inspiration, and the ineffably important *stick-to-it-ness* that makes it possible for you to complete your *real* work, the *absorbedness,* as poet Donald Hall calls it, to disappear into the work. The old mountain man stood his ground, as we all should when we're challenged about our creative urges. He stayed focused, as in near his fire, as we should try to do. He remained rooted in his belief, as we can only hope to do.

This fifth stage of the creative journey—focusing—throws more people than any other. Who isn't distracted by our hyped-up world? Who doesn't feel the latest statistics, which tell us that the average person is assaulted by over 1000 advertisements a day. Our excuses for not working at any given time are legion. We mumble to ourselves or to friends about money problems, time issues, supplies, depression, emails, car problems, or the neighbor's parrot being so loud that we can't concentrate. There is always something else to do, someone else to meet, another book to read, a party to attend, an old movie to watch, dishes to do, closets to clean. "The frightening thing," Jean Renoir observed in *The Rules of the Game,* "is that everybody has their reasons."

What are your reasons? If you've read this far in the book, you're fascinated by the ferment in your soul, but you may be frustrated by what you've actually accomplished. You want to redouble your effort, but you're stuck. Maybe you've lost your fire, your splendid fierceness. What's keeping you from focusing on your work? What will it take for *you* to move?

Over the years, I've been consulted on hundreds of projects that were dead in the water—often because these creative people were simply so busy with other things that they couldn't concentrate long enough to keep their book or film or painting moving forward. I know a painter who got lonely and put a small black-and-white TV next to his easel to keep him company. Slowly but surely, he became addicted to the distraction and his daily painting time diminished to almost nothing. He ended up having to cancel a major exhibition. I was once consulted by a well-to-do banker about his stillborn novel. When I arrived at his office, I found two stacks of papers on his desk: one of banking papers and the other the pages of his unfinished novel. His wife didn't like him writing during "family time," so he was trying to write for an hour or two after work. I advised him to find the time and the place and the will to focus on his work—whichever work he chose.

No one said it would be easy. If it was, it wouldn't be creative. If it were easy, anybody could do it. The question is always whether or not you can focus when it's *hard going*.

EXERCISE 11. Seven Ways to Improve Your Focus

What is worthy of your attention? Remember: it's not what you see, it's how you see it, and whether it sees you. What is worthy of your attention? List three things you feel could be worthy of your time. Now make something out of one of them—a story, a song, a sketch.

What's the song for? What's the job it's supposed to do? These two poignant questions posed by folksinger Pete Seeger helped Bruce Springsteen focus on returning to his roots-sound for the album *Magic*. They can help you, too.

List three things you know distract you from your work. Return to the list and *let go* of one more thing.

Can you block out the trivial? Cut out the frivolous? Think about the trivial pursuits that are taking up your time. Think of ways you can "create time" by eliminating these activities from your day.

How long can you stick with the work? Do you have stick-to-it-ness? Keep track of how long you work at your creative project each day. Make a note of what made you stop working, then write down something you could have done to avoid the distraction. Finally, focus on focused people.

Buy a special clock just for your creative work space. Set the alarm for concentrated periods of focused work—a half hour, an hour, then two hours. Find your comfortable capacity for work. Make a habit out of it.

Find a group of kindred spirits. Years ago, while doing a long stint of housepainting, I joined a James Joyce book club, which met every Friday night at The Albatross Pub in Berkeley. Those evenings saved me from losing my way; they helped me incubate my ideas for a few years until I was ready to start writing again. Cormac McCarthy joined the Santa Fe Institute for companionship and intellectual stimulation, and also research for his post-apocalypse novel *The Road*. Seek out and join the group that would help you get back in sync with the ideas and passions that first made you want to be an artist.

"ATTENTION MUST BE PAID"

Surely these words of Arthur Miller in *Death of a Salesman* are among the most prophetic of our time. The question for us is what they mean for our creative journeys. I'm reminded of the ominous billboard in San Francisco that, a few years ago, blared the virtues of being "connected" 24/7/365, insinuating that, if you're *not* connected everywhere, all the time, you can't possibly be successful. Surely, not hip.

Well, that's certainly one ideal. But I have another one in mind.

Fortunately, you won't find it on billboards or computer screens. You only find it in the careful observation of creative people whose focus helps reveal the richest range of human capacity for attention, even devotion, to important work. I'm convinced this is one of the deep fascinations we have with artists, athletes, scientists, and mystics. Of course, we're impressed with their talent; but it is their *deep focus* on a project or a cause that inspires us.

Goethe focused on *Faust* for sixty years; Lance Armstrong brought ferocious concentration to his sport eight hours a day, six days a week, year after year until he finally won the Tour de France—then triumphed six more times before retiring. Martha Graham sat through all-night rituals and dance ceremonies of the Navajo and Hopi in the belief that stirring her own "blood memories" of the human race would trigger a vision. Creative people seem to possess a fifth gear that lets them see a broader vision, go for long periods without sleep or food, and ignore things that don't pertain to their passion.

Maybe that's why I've always had a gallery of "focus heroes." As a kid, I was fascinated by Greenfield Village, where Henry Ford had moved the homes and shops of famous inventors such as Thomas Edison and the Wright Brothers. I grew up immersed in their stories of persistence in the face of failure, and their ultimate triumph. I was fascinated by the intense focus of the skaters at the Ice Capades and the steelworkers around the blast furnaces in Detroit. Later, when I lived in Dublin, I became obsessed with the physical agonies of my first literary hero, James Joyce, who endured thirteen eye operations, but still stayed focused enough to write *Ulysses,* the most revolutionary novel of the 20th century. As I grew older, I acquired new heroes: Newton, who took thirty years to work out his theories of gravitation; Cervantes and Marco Polo, who told their tales in prison; Luke Howard, an amateur meteorologist who labored for twenty-two years on his unprecedented cataloging of cloud shapes; Lionel Poilâne, the Parisian philosopher-baker who saw the French soul in his loaves of bread.

But we can also find extraordinary focus in the most ordinary people and places. We just have to learn to recognize life's lessons when they're handed to us. When I met Monsieur Poilâne, he proudly told me how his father had bartered bread for paintings with artists too poor to buy food—the young Picasso and Braque. "What matters," he told me with his eyes caressing the loaves baking in the ancient brick ovens, "is the magic of the hands. We are a culture of hands and eyes, which is, perhaps, why we value beauty so highly."

Torch singer Peggy Lee once said that she picked up her wisdom along the dusty road of life: "I learned how to live from Jesus, Cary Grant, and the Buddha." I too take my models wherever I find them—artists, athletes, mechanics, and scientists. One night many years ago, I rode up into the Berkeley hills to view the Perseid meteor showers. There, under a dark scrim of sky scratched with the silver tracks of glorious meteors, a sidewalk astronomer taught me the secret of seeing with "soft eyes." Peer just to the left or right of the star you're trying to see, he told me. It's all a matter of focus.

Writer's Block. Shadow box art by Michael Ferreboeuf, 2003.

Who knows when and where we relearn how to focus? One night in a San Francisco bar, I was having a beer with Michael Ferreboeuf, the headmaster of nearby Cathedral School for Boys. He confided to me that his abiding passion was "shadow box art." His fascination began in his grandparents' basement. "That was the spark, the genesis for me," he said. "All that stuff in their basement *had life to it.* I believe inanimate objects have *presence* and that it's *retrievable* if I collect it, frame it, photograph it. I feel as if I'm preserving more than history; I'm preserving stories and lives." So he would scour yard sales, antique shops, and estate sales for objects like old watches, baseballs, and records, and then preserve them through his art. Focus, concentration, attention. It's just this side of obsession; it's a survival instinct, and there is no creative work without it. Distracted people make no masterpieces. Trendy people leave no permanent mark. What saves you is your soul's recognition of the work that will tell you who you are. As French filmmaker Jean Cocteau said: "[the] task is to keep alive the flame—or everything goes to ashes." One afternoon, in the late 1970s, I encountered a live example of that fiery metaphor. I was hiking through Muir Woods, when I passed the startling sight of the dancer Rudolph Nureyev sitting on a redwood tree stump. He wore a black beret and a black felt cape. He sat stockstill, gazing off into space, as if visualizing every leap and spin of the performance he was going to deliver later that night at the Opera House in San Francisco. As I looked back at him, it occurred to me he was trying to *will* the performance to life. Since then I've often thought about that magical moment among the redwoods, usually when I was about to lecture or go on camera.

EXERCISE 12. A Simple Focus Practice

Walk down your street as if you were passing along it for the first time and notice one new thing that catches your attention. Let's say the mosaics on the school entrance. Now close your eyes. See it in your mind's eye. Open your eyes. Focus. Close. Sense your way in. Take out your notebook and write about or draw it in detail. When you think you've described it fully, don't fool yourself; do it again. Go deeper in your description; use more detail, open your perceptions to color, light, materials, and the way the building or structure or object connects to everything around it—or doesn't. Now ask yourself what this building or object says about the neighborhood, the city, the nation. Was the person who created it focused? Are people focused on it now, or is it merely background?

It is always a revelation to me how an appreciation of my surroundings can influence the way I focus on ideas, thoughts, and objects. *Everything* can be a point of focus. We just have to discipline ourselves to perceive more deeply and appreciate more fully. The result is a fuller life.

What I'm calling for here isn't easy. The only answer to the question of focus is what helps you concentrate—what motivates you to "pay attention," as Miller enjoined us. So many distractions, so little time. But creative people always have their ways of "paying attention." Jackson Pollack was notorious for painting while listening to raucous jazz as he worked in the tight quarters of a barn. Canadian folk singer Gordon Lightfoot disappears into the absolute silence of an all-white-painted cabin in the remote wilds of the Yukon to write his songs. Photographer Wilson Bentley, in a rhapsody on the theme of deep focus and fascination, wearied of shooting landscapes and ended up focusing on snowflakes, some 50,000 of them etched on glass plates. It's all a matter of discipline and focus on what we alone, sometimes, may save from being lost.

For me, the most soulful family ritual my parents created in our home when I was growing up was reading out loud together. Over the years we managed—with each of us taking a page at a time—to read classics like Homer's *Odyssey,* Mark Twain's *Huckleberry Finn,* and Charles Nordhoff's *Mutiny on the Bounty.* One winter, when I was around ten, my father brought home a Heritage Club edition of Jack London's *To Build a Fire.* As the snow fell, we read:

> *The old-timer had been very serious in laying down the law that no man should travel alone in the Klondike after fifty below . . . There was the*

fire, snapping and crackling and promising life
with every dancing flame . . . He cherished the
flame carefully and awkwardly. It meant life, and
it must not perish . . .

To my young ears and eyes, the author's descriptions of the miner's hands and toes going numb, the snow on the cedar branches falling onto the fragile fire, the last of the matches flaring and dying, were partly literary, partly mythological. As E. L. Doctorow has recently pointed out, the nameless miner's dilemma has become a kind of parable—a warning story for everyone on a risky adventure to learn how to keep your matches dry and how to light a fire without singeing your hands.

It's strange how often, over the years, this simple but vivid story has crystallized in my mind, usually when I feel stuck in some do-or-die drama. You may already know how easily the fire goes out and, worse, how many people are perversely willing to turn the fire hose on your flames.

In the early 1960s in a lecture at the Cooper Union Hall in New York, Joseph Campbell was asked what you should do if you are stuck in your life. "Follow your fascination," he immediately replied. Your fascination reveals your deepest connection to the life force; if you follow it rather than what society tells you you should follow, you will be all right.

EXERCISE 13. Five Ways to Follow Your Fascination

One point a day. Choosing one focus, one theme, one idea a day is a time-tested way to corral your wild-horse imagination. Carry a camera and take one photo, and one only, over the course of a day.

Learn to say "no." Trying to please everybody all the time is a guaranteed way to lose track of your real work. Saying no allows you to concentrate on what you need to say yes to.

Nail something on your wall that will remind you to say *yes* to life. Art critic Michael Kimmelman recommends we do this with prints of Wayne Thiebaud's joyous paintings.

Cultivate your brooding. To brood means "to bring to life." The fact that it's become a pejorative term ("Stop brooding, Johnny!") betrays the common suspicion that brooding keeps people from working and may lead to Johnny becoming . . . an artist!

Honor Hestia, goddess of the hearth, where our original focus once faced. If possible, build a fire or light a candle, gaze into a fireplace. Focusing on the

Poulnabrone Dolmen, Ireland. Pencil sketch by Phil Cousineau, 2002.

flames of a real fire has the uncanny ability to help us later on focus on what needs to be done.

Gaze into the distance, the mountains, the ocean, the sky. "Take in some distant horizon," as travel writer Bruce Chatwin was advised by his eye doctor. It affords us new perspectives.

What does focus mean to you? How long can you focus? Do you dare lose yourself in your concentration practice? Can you focus at will? How easily are you pulled away by your children, the telephone, the mail, the television, the dishes, the books not being in alphabetical order? With whom do you identify when you think about deeply focused work? Are you like Tom Sawyer focusing his magnifying glass on insects?

Do you have the ability to focus on the larger picture of history—like Gandhi sitting for fourteen hours in a South African train station, which his granddaughter once described to me as "his most creative moment" because that was the day he committed to *Satyagraha,* a life of nonviolence? Do you have the patience of Lady Gregory sitting for hours around the smoky peat fires of West Ireland collecting and writing down old Irish fairy tales from the last of the *seanachies?* Are you like the sculptress Barbara Hepworth, who was fond of running her hands over every vein of stone for hours before going to work? Or like cartoonist Chuck Jones, creator of rabbit hero Bugs Bunny, who reread Mark Twain's *Adventures of Huckleberry Finn* every year to remind himself of the inherent morality of rebel characters? No matter how you choose to be creative, "attention must be paid."

THE FAR SIDE OF FOCUS

Stuart Balcomb is a musician, composer, and editor of *The Scream*, an online literary magazine. Writing to me of the role of focus in his career, he says:

> *My concepts often come as whole packages, with endings already in place. I once worked as a music copyist on* Indiana Jones and the Temple of Doom *at 20th Century Fox (this was in the days when we wrote by hand—before computer notation programs). Four of us worked almost all day to complete six piccolo parts for the final chase scene, which was one of the busiest and most complex pieces of music I've ever had to work on. My eyes were burning at the end of the day, and on the way home I had an idea for a self-portrait, complete with many eyeballs, slaving over a score. In spite*

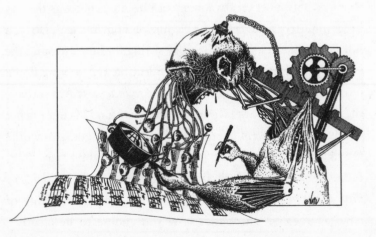

Self-Portrait, pen & ink. Artwork copyright © 1984 by Stuart Vail Balcomb.

of my red and aching eyes, I did the pencil sketch
for the drawing before I went to bed that night.

It takes a great *effort* to focus on your manuscript, painting, or music—the effort that is no effort at all if you love what you do. Take it from Calvin and Hobbes. The magical tiger asks the little explorer why he's digging a hole in the backyard and learns the boy's looking for treasure and has found "dirty rocks, a weird root, and some disgusting grubs . . . There's treasure everywhere!"

DEEP FOCUS IN A NUTSHELL

Your focus is what you actually pay attention to.
Your best concentration is on your fascination.
Visualize your ideas through inner focus—then
realize them through outer focus.

WHERE IS YOUR FOCUS POINT NOW?

Is it on your project or on the ten
thousand daily distractions?

Can you commit to a daily focus practice?

The Personification of Agon. Bronze statue of a Young Male Athlete,
second century B.C.E., National Archaeological Museum, Athens, Greece.
Photograph by Phil Cousineau, 2004.

CHAPTER 7

Burn-Out

Stop stewing. It's unserious of you. We all get stuck. The thing is to get unstuck. Come to my island. Lillian.

—Lillian Hellman to Peter Feibleman

In 1984, I was asked by Tony Joseph, a noted San Francisco scholar of mythology and astrology, to co-lead an art and literary tour to Ireland with poet Robert Bly and storyteller Gioia Timpanelli. We spent the first night in Ennis at a 200-year-old inn, the Olde Ground Hotel. After dinner, we rounded out the evening with the old tour ritual of going around the room and allowing everyone a few minutes to introduce themselves.

One man in his late thirties with a cool air about him introduced himself simply as John, and said he was a drummer who played music for years in "an L.A. band." After the session,

I invited him for a pint in the inn's renowned Poet's Bar, where Joyce, Synge, Yeats, Kavanaugh, and others had all tossed back a drink or two while writing verses or reciting bawdy limericks. Eventually, John revealed that he hadn't been in just any band; he was John Densmore, drummer for The Doors. For the next few hours, we traded tales like kids with rare baseball cards—my stories of working with Joseph Campbell and his life with the poet-shaman Lizard King, Jim Morrison. During our conversation, he shyly mentioned he had begun to write his memoirs.

Later that fall, I rang him up and asked if he'd like me to look over his manuscript. After poring over the forty or so pages at his spectacular home in Bel-Air, I ran a few ideas by him about how he might restructure the book—excavating some of the old stories, adding some social details about the sixties, and speculating about the mythology of rock and roll. Mostly, I encouraged him to tell his electrifying story from his own unique point of view—as a drummer, behind the band, watching the entire Doors saga unfold. He hired me on the spot to help him "break on through" and finish the book.

The next morning, we dug into the manuscript. Wanting to start out on an upbeat note, I asked him to rap about the day his close friend and Doors lead guitar player, Robbie Krieger, brought in the first two verses for the song that became the anthem of a generation, "Light My Fire." The next few hours unfolded like a dream. I learned firsthand about the kinetic energy of a band on the knife's edge between greatness and madness. It was like looking behind the Wizard's curtain in Oz to hear about how Krieger's lyrics inspired Manzarek's classic organ opening, which in turn triggered Densmore's own soft jazz flourish on drums, and how Morrison disappeared into the studio bathroom where he wrote the third verse of the song in five minutes.

However, it wasn't long before the glamorous tales devolved into stories of tension, competition, and self-destruction—mostly Morrison's. My searing impression from working with John for five years on the book that became *Riders on the Storm* was that Morrison's career echoed Charles Dickens' famous opening to *A Tale of Two Cities:* "They were the best of times and the worst of times." For John, the last years of the band were a tragic waste of time and talent. By the time The Doors finished their last studio album in 1970, Morrison was "torched," as John put it. He was drinking outrageously, overweight, angry, disappointed in himself, the group, and "the scene" in America. Three months after flying off to Paris "to finish the great American novel," he was dead of an apparent drug overdose at the impossibly young age of 27. Many years later, the band's manager, Danny Sugerman, confided to me on the real reason for Morrison's untimely death:

> *His life reminds me of something Jung once asked himself, "Are you living the myth or is the myth living you?" It sounds to me like the myth took over . . . He was flirting with death all along, dancing on fire. Maybe he thought he could outwit death. In the end, Jim just plain burned himself out.*

A TOUCH OF MADNESS

The story, of course, doesn't end there. Jim Morrison was a brilliant poet and an electrifying performer, a rock 'n' roll icon.

But he's also become the poster boy for self-destruction, the transcendent symbol for burning out rather than fading away. He's our modern Chatterton, Byron, and Rimbaud all rolled into one pair of tight leather pants. He's the incarnation of Jack London's famous cry: "I would rather that my spark burn out in a brilliant blaze than it should be stifled by dry rot . . . I shall not waste my days in trying to prolong them. I shall use my time."

"Cautionary tales abound," says Jeff "The Dude" Dowd. From lives like theirs, we learn the painful truth that the fires of creativity can be all-consuming. It's an old story. Plato wrote that genius was not without a touch of madness. His theory of "Platonic madness" was revived in the Renaissance

Memento vitae, Memento mori, frieze, San Francisco, California. Photograph by Phil Cousineau, 1981.

as a belief that artists were born under the sign of Saturn, the planet of melancholia. Philosophers described the temperament of painters, sculptors, and poets as contemplative, solitary, and obsessive—but also sinister, depressive, and brooding.

Three centuries later, Romantic notions of "sacred madness" and "divine enthusiasm" resurfaced in the lives of poets like Shelley and Keats, later Woolf and Churchill, who described his depression as a "Black Dog" that mercilessly hounded him. In modern times, the belief that creativity is a bittersweet gift from the gods has been personified by innumerable novelists, poets, artists, and actors—from Sylvia Plath's "blood jets of poetry" to Janis Joplin's "Every night I make love to a thousand people—and then go home alone." Herman Melville's late onset of corrosive melancholy and self-doubt prevented him from writing for the last forty years of his life. J. D. Salinger has suffered from a four-decade-long writer's block. Harper Lee hasn't written anything since *To Kill a Mockingbird*. Ralph Ellison never finished the sequel to *The Invisible Man*.

What leads to burn-out like this? What are the warning signs for someone hitting rock bottom? Is there a pattern the rest of us can decipher so we can learn from other's harrowing hell? Why can some creative people rekindle their fires over and over, while others have a fast-burning fuse in their souls that dooms them to explosion or implosion some time in mid life?

For some creative souls, the downward spiral may be caused by chemical imbalance, as with Sylvia Plath, William Saroyan, or Van Gogh. For others, it may be social, as with those whose skills have deteriorated because of political repression, like my friend the Cambodian poet and monk U Sam

Oeur, who feigned silence and ignorance during the scourge of the Khmer Rouge so he could survive, see his wife again, and write his *Sacred Vows*.

The soul has a million mechanisms for telling you to stop, for warning you you're headed in the wrong direction. The sixth stage of your creative journey can end either in bitter disappointment—or in the sounding of your soul's alarm that something's killing your creativity and that you must *turn around*—or else. As Dick Bolles, author of *What Color is Your Parachute?* told me recently, "If you're lost on your journey, you *must* find a new center."

THE WORK IS THE WAY OUT

Where are you in this picture? Are you stuck because you're burned out? Sick of your project, though it's hard to admit? Are you ready to implode or explode? If so, join the crowd. You'd be surprised how many creative people struggle with the dragon of self-doubt, the depression of rejection, the sense of being immolated like the phoenix. It can be shocking to learn how many novels languish unfinished in somebody's desk drawer, how many movies are never released, how many paintings go unsold, how many songs unheard.

Failure in the creative world is a lot like baseball batting averages. Three hits in ten at-bats may sound pretty weak to those outside of baseball, but for those in the know, a .300 batting average can earn you kudos and million-dollar contracts. Similarly, in the creative world, everybody who picks up a pen, camera, brush, guitar, chisel, or carving knife knows how many false starts, dead ends, and nasty criticisms are just part of the game. The redoubtable Thomas Edison responded to flattery about his famous 10,000 patents by saying, "Yes, but for every one of those patents there were 10,000 more failed experiments." Mary Pickford, the silent movie actress, understood. "Failure is not falling down," she said, "it's staying down."

I thought of this when I visited the Agon exhibition in Athens during the 2004 Olympics. The agon was the contest, the competition, the rivalry in sports, war, business and relationships, giving rise to our words for athlete and also agony. The struggle to perform well, the Greeks taught, is agonizing, but the only way to achieve excellence, which is the hallmark of the well-lived life.

For some, the stumbling block is the pursuit of perfection, which may feel like a guiding light in the heart of the writer or painter, but to those observing is an exercise in futility or vanity. While we all want to excel, the question is whether the twentieth draft of a chapter is still polishing, or if it's a failure of will to finally stand by your work. I know an inventor-artist in Sintra, Portugal, who has been working on a "perpetual motion machine-and-neon sculpture," for over thirty years. He vaunts it as an astounding combination of technological wizardry and artistic vision. The trouble is he's been slaving away on it for three decades and never shown it to a single human soul. His story is a perfect, though painful, example of the pressing question we should all ask ourselves: *What are we waiting for?*

When asked by a student how he'd ever know if he'd finished a painting, Salvador Dalí warned: "Don't worry about perfection; you'll never get there." Good advice. The ill-fated pursuit of perfection in creative works seems to be a sin of literalism—the *literalization* of the pursuit of *excellence,* the all-or-nothing, competitive striving for victory at all costs. Whether there's confusion between the noble pursuit of scientific rigor and the search for beautiful artistic metaphors, or an eye focused, not on contemporary success, but on immortal fame, the result is the same. The quest for perfection is a tortuous one that leads to anguish, torture, and often long periods of lassitude and noncreativity. Burn-out, by any other name.

How can you step by from the edge of this burn-out? Is there another way to deal with this fear? Can anger be a catalyst, a motivator, even self-protection? Here are ten ways to break out of a futile quest for perfection so you can complete your creative journey. The darkest place is right behind the candle.

EXERCISE 14. Ten Ways to Step Back from the Edge

Never do any work that makes you feel guilty.

Slowly and kindly, let go of the negative people in your life.

Share your fears, your anxiety, your doubt, then let them go. Your downtime might be incubation.

Face criticism boldly; never fear either failure or life.

Remember artmaking isn't selfish; it's a contribution.

Change is hell. So is overwork. All work and no play make Jack and Jill very uncreative kids.

Refrain from calling yourself an author, actor, or artist, as I heard Robert Bly remark at a conference in 1982. I believe he meant that nouns inflate while verbs deflate. Instead, he suggested we say simply: I write, I act, I paint. A great burden will fall from your shoulders.

Resist the siren calls of fame.

Take care of yourself. Stay active. Poor health leads to loss of energy and festering anger.

Be original; not trendy. To be original, be honest.

Never succumb to the illusion of entitlement. Be grateful for anything positive that comes from your work.

At a conference in Atlanta in 2004, I sat in on an informal talk about myth and creativity given by the prolific author Joyce Carol Oates, who described two of her prime motivations: long-distance running and boxing matches (yes, boxing matches). Running, she claimed, gives her ideas; boxing matches give her an image of failure that spurs her to succeed. Pugnacious, but powerful advice.

Those of us who've hovered—afraid, fearful, and angry—at the threshold of what I've come to think of as *the real work*—the work we were summoned into this life to do— have to commit to rekindling the soul's fire. We have to remind ourselves every day that there will *always* be prodigious powers to work against us as we pursue worthy goals or attempt transformation. It's not what happens *to* you, it's what happens *in* you, what you do with what happens to you—in your work and your relationships—that really matters.

Is there a way out of the labyrinth, the belly of the whale, the bottom of the bottle? Is there a way to stoke the creative fire even when you can't see the fireplace for all the smoke in the room? How do you find the hot embers in your own cold heart?

EXERCISE 15. Three Ways to Rekindle Your Fire

Follow the thread back to your original fire. The French writer Albert Camus' advice was simple and elegant: "Return to the one or two images that first

Example of Healing Art. *When You Play Soccer You Don't Think about Your Allergies.* Chalk on paper by Renan Andrade Costa Pereira, age eleven, Sao Paulo, Brazil, 2007. Courtesy of Dr. Roberto Takaoka.

opened up [your] heart." Wiser words have rarely been said. There is something powerful in this advice, something mythological, a parallel to the ageless story of the hero slaying the dragon in the cave and releasing the life-affirming force that heals the wasteland. As Kierkegaard wrote: "Life must be lived forwards but understood backwards." Identify two events in your life that set you on your creative path. Then make a list of all the things in your life these events have influenced.

Find your inner Robinson Crusoe. I've been intrigued with the timeless story of Robinson Crusoe for years, because it offers an example of the difference between solitude and loneliness. Though Crusoe spent years alone on his island, there is very little evidence in the book that he was lonely. Was he lonely or content? True creativity demands a great deal of time alone, which means sacrificing time with others. The Crusoe complex, as I think of it, is an important consideration in the creative journey, because it raises to the forefront the issue of time alone, which society discourages but is still essential to the creative life. Most creative projects require a painful amount of time alone. Are you up to it? Or is the isolation corrosive? Is there a way to assuage the discomfort? Think about ways you can set aside "time alone" without negatively impacting your other relationships. *Now make something out of it, again.*

Visualize Buster Keaton in *The General* when he survives the wall of a house falling on him. In this famous stunt Keaton stands in the one and only place he can survive when the house crashes down all around him—the exact space of a small, open window. Recall his definition of three-act structure: Disaster, Survival, Surprise. Likewise, every art project flirts with danger. Try to imagine placing yourself in such a way that you avoid being burned, crushed, or demolished as the world seemingly falls all around you.

The work is the way out. The work is the thread. Don't think about it. Don't talk about it. Don't theorize about it. Just do it. Do the work—as in the *working,* the writing of the poem, the sketching of the portrait, the composing of the concerto. The work is the way out.

So I ask you now: How's your fire? How's your heart? Are you able to move on? Or are you burned out? Fried? Torched? Are you toying with the idea of quitting? For now? Forever? If you're flirting with the idea of putting off some creative work, ask yourself: What do I have to do to continue on my creative journey? Do I have the courage to carry on? How can I *spark* the fire.

And maybe the most important question of all: What will it take for me to move on? The only way to navigate through is to put up your sails. The only way out of the labyrinth is to never let go of the thread. The thread led you this far, and it will lead you on. The only way to continue the journey is to keep on keepin' on.

IF YOU'RE STUCK, STRETCH

Sound when stretched is music.
Movement when stretched is dance.
Mind when stretched is meditation.
Life when stretched is celebration.

—*Ravi Shankar*

KEEP ON KEEPIN' ON

What most of us fear is not failure, its attempting the impossible. John Ruskin, the famed literary critic, once told the tale of a passenger aboard a sinking ship who fastened 200 pounds of gold around his waist so it wouldn't be lost at sea. He was found later at the bottom of the ocean. Now, as he was sinking, Ruskin asked, "Did he have the gold or did the gold have him?" I've asked myself that same question more than once. Is the "gold" in this work going to save me, or take me down with it because I'm ruining my health or relationships?

While visiting an old friend, Julia Clotworthy, at her home in Bath, England, I found myself skimming the titles on her bookshelves. I came across a copy of Aldous Huxley's essays and opened it to one entitled *Why I Write,* which Huxley had completed during the London blitzkrieg. These blistering words jumped out at me: "Writing a book is a horrible, exhausting struggle, like a long bout of some painful illness. One would never undertake such a thing if one were not driven on by some demon who one cannot resist or understand." The words struck me to the core. I don't think Huxley was writing about the cartoonish devil of traditional religion; I think he was writing about the one we all confront when we pursue the deepest and darkest truths of our lives—the *daemon,* the second soul, the force that can paralyze or catalyze us.

I know this daemon only too well.

Once, after years spent writing for local newspapers, the creative fire in me went out. I'd gone through a number of difficult personal and family experiences that may have contributed to my loss of creative energy. Whatever the reason, the fire sputtered and went out. I spent the next few years traveling the back roads of the world, filling dozens of notebooks with my experiences, building a cache of ideas and memories that I just couldn't seem to turn into creative works. Whenever I feel stuck on a creative project now, I think back on those years and the fear of repeating them serves as an impetus to work as hard as I can on my books, films, lectures, and coaching. I think it's this *constructive fear*—the healthy fear of fire that saves the life of the firefighter, the fear of an inside fastball that makes a batter flinch just in time—that keeps me from getting stuck again in that same unproductive, uncreative rut. In my case, it's the fairly terrifying fear, which ricochets back at me in dream life about once a year, of being flung back into that prior life that provides a curious source of motivation. While I'm not recommending you induce fear as a spur to creativity, I can stand by its effectiveness. What I do recommend is that you live by one simple rule: "*Move, move, move.*"

It may sound counterintuitive, but my reading of the biographies of creative people and a constant review of my own life and work has shown me that, when you reach the darkest part of the forest, it means you're halfway home. You have to keep going. When I'm suffering from a case of debilitating depression or procrastination, what works for me is to *get darker*—at least until it gets light again. For me, that means playing adagio music while I'm trying to get back into the groove, watching war movies, reading crime novels, going to blues bars. Whatever it takes; just don't give in.

After working for seven years on my epic poem about famous last words, *Deadlines,* I nearly threw it into the fireplace. After spending two years, day and night, working on *The Peyote Road,* my collaborator Gary Rhine and I nearly threw in the towel. After writing for sixteen hours a day for six months to finish *The Olympic Odyssey,* I almost caved in to exhaustion. But in every case, I "kept on keepin' on," as we used to say on the streets of Detroit. I lifted my glass and shouted out the old Aussie toast, "Press on, regardless." Call it what you will— pride, stubbornness, momentum, or determination—there was also an ineffable force at work—the old-fashioned belief in destiny, the feeling that this is what I'm supposed to do with my life. Each project felt like a long race I couldn't possibly quit, or a love affair I couldn't give up on.

EXERCISE 16. Four Ways to Keep on Keepin' On

Practice the art of the *aperçu.* Quick inspiration, lush-n-lambent, brief survey or sketch, immediate impression, especially insights. When exhausted or drained, it's important to rest, but then to start up again at a reasonable pace. Sit in a busy place and take "snapshot" impressions of the people who pass by. Write down three salient characteristics of each person. Think about why those characteristics struck you.

Trust your ability to improvise, as Edward Hopper did when he couldn't "get any idea for a picture." He sketched and sketched and sketched until something clicked. One such drawing, which he didn't think much of at the time, later transformed into *Gas,* one of his greatest oil paintings.

Practice the art of the *pocheaus*. It was an old trick of the Impressionists to take portable water colors with them into the countryside and make quick-studies. Go for a long walk and take a small note-book. Write or draw quick studies of three objects or people you encounter. Think about why you chose these subjects.

Think of every flare as an ember to be coaxed into flame. Send someone in trouble, someone lonely and unmotivated, an inspiring letter. Recently this came by email to me: "Start by doing what's necessary, then what's possible, and suddenly you are doing the impossible." Do the impossible—start over, stoke your creative fire. Stir yourself.

In the late 1990s, I was approached by Bob Cooper, a World War II veteran whose dream was to write a biography of fighter pilot and memoirist Bert Stiles. By the time we met, Cooper had already done a great deal of original research—as

I soon learned, perhaps too much. After a two-hour consultation, it became clear that the sheer volume of material was intimidating; the more he read of other pilots, the more doubts he had about his own project. He had lost his way; his fire was fading; he was in danger of losing his enthusiasm for the book. What I recommended was simple. I told him he was burned out because the original work had been smothered by the weight of his research; no oxygen could get in to keep the flames alive. He had to let some fresh air into the project.

As is often the case, he'd forgotten why he began the book in the first place. So I suggested that he go to a neutral place, get out of his writing studio for a day or a weekend, and review Stiles' early writings and press clippings. I told him to write *himself* a letter to remind himself why he had started the project. Go see Stiles' family, I told him, and get recharged from their memories. Go deeper. Find out if Stiles had a shadow side. Ask yourself why you're really doing this book. Can you live without it? When I asked him this, his face went white. No, he couldn't face life without it. He was hooked. I vowed to help him see it through. With encouragement from his wife and the Stiles family, Cooper revived the book and published it in late 2002.

When I asked the composer Stuart Balcomb how he dealt with the inevitable dark nights of the soul in his prolific career, he answered:

> *I've certainly had my moments. I was scoring an episode of the Batman animated series in 1993. I had worked a solid week writing the music, and it was about midnight before the recording session.*

All the other scores had been delivered to War-
ner Bros., the parts copied and booked up for
the players, and I had only one last cue to write.
The problem was that I was completely drained.
Exhausted and creatively spent, I could not go any
further. I stared at the empty score pages that I
had prepared and wondered what to do. I briefly
entertained the idea of running away, booking
a flight somewhere. It then suddenly hit me that
A) the earth turns and tomorrow will come, and
B) at 10:00 tomorrow I will be standing on the
podium in front of an orchestra with a baton in
my hand, ready to give a downbeat, and all these
pages will be filled in, black with notes. I visual-
ized the future. It was tomorrow and the task was
done. All I had to do was get from here to there.
And at that moment all the ideas started to flow.
That visualization made the process much easier,
and I've used it ever since.

EXERCISE 17. Six Ways to Avoid Burn-out

Remember that creativity allows for mistakes. Recall
what Edison once admitted, that he had 10,000 patents, but also 10,000 failures for each one. Visualize
your project as completed, then work your way back
through the steps that got you there. Use this as a
plan for moving forward.

"You must praise the mutilated world," suggests
Polish writer Adam Zagajewski. This startling line

contains a multitude of meanings, not the least of which is that it challenges us to put our sorrows into perspective. Explore what it means to you.

Forgive yourself. It's impossible to love your work if you don't love yourself. Write down three things that you are fiercely proud of in your work.

Put a curfew on your own work hours. Always leave a few embers glowing for the next day's work.

Create a firewall. This can be the one or two inexhaustible works of art that make you believe life itself is worthwhile: Mozart's piano concertos, Moore's mobiles, Cassatt's children. Return to these works whenever your fire is fading.

Don't worry about failure. Remember Bob Dylan still feels "unfulfilled" because he never became a movie usher. Everyone feels the wound of an unmet dream.

THE PHOENIX, THE POET, AND PERSEPHONE RISING

The phoenix is a mythological creature of rebirth, a fantastic feathered bird that bursts into flames, then flares back to life from its own ashes. "The phoenix stands for constancy," wrote da Vinci. "When it wishes to be renewed, according to its nature, it is constant in its endurance of the burning flames which consume it, and then it is reborn once more." That's the very definition of *burning curiosity*. To understand this— perhaps to believe it—I go rummaging around the world for

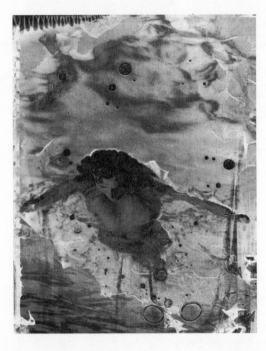

Persephone Rising.
Polaroid wet-negative
transfer by Joanne
Warfield, 2001.

stones to strike the flint of my imagination, like Coleridge who
went daily to the British Museum because, he said, he was "a
scavenger for metaphors."

I like—maybe I *need*—illustrations of creative people
coming back to life, phoenix-like. I seek out artists who beat
their wings over the nearly dead embers of their own imagina-
tions. I think of Mark Twain, stuck for seven years in the middle
of *Huckleberry Finn* at the point where Huck and Jim lose their
way looking for the Ohio River. On some intuitive level, he
knew that if he took a steamboat up the Ohio, he would be able
to visualize the rest of the book. That trip ignited the phoenix force in his soul and spurred him to finish his masterpiece.
Bruce Bochte, a major league first baseman, felt this phoenix

force in his soul when, after leaving the game in mid career in protest over the league going on strike, he volunteered to work with an organization dedicated to saving Seattle Bay. Recently, he told me that year renewed his love for baseball and gave him a vision for his life after retiring. Out of a desperate situation, he saw the larger picture and found a way to revive his spark. Bochte's story ignited a fire in me when I first heard it. I realized that apparent fame and riches—in art, politics, or sports—can be an illusion. There are a remarkable number of ways that human beings can make themselves successful and productive.

One of my own most moving experiences of the phoenix force in my own soul occurred when I was working on my book on Joseph Campbell, *Soul: An Archaeology*. I was feeling slack and deeply depressed about my inability to circumnavigate that vast territory. I needed a jolt. While jogging one morning, I chanced on a playbill for Eugene O'Neill's *Long Day's Journey into Night* and knew immediately that I had to go. Near the end of act four, young Edmund (speaking for O'Neill) describes an evening at sea:

> *I became drunk with the beauty and singing rhythm of it, and for a moment I lost myself—actually lost my life. I was set free! I dissolved in the sea, became white sails and flying spray, became beauty and rhythm, became moonlight and ship and the high, dim-starred sky! I belonged, without past or future, within peace and unity and a wild joy, within something greater than my own life, or the life of Man, to Life itself.*

The Tree of Life, Casa Grande, Arizona. Photograph by Phil Cousineau, 2006.

It's hard for me to convey what those lines did to me. There was a blazing fire in every word. I lost myself in the telling—the first sign of reverie. Leaving the theater, I had to walk for hours, as if in shock. As is the case in sublime works of art, the artist had captured what I'd been secretly feeling. That passage and that performance gave me the courage of my convictions. Reverie isn't only real; it may be the most real thing about us. Moreover, O'Neill showed me that, through some still undiscovered alchemy, one man's reverie can be another's recovery. O'Neill's, mine, maybe yours. The creative life may be dangerous because it exposes us to ridicule and disapproval, but it is still the boldest move we can make with the talent we bring into this world. The trick, if there is one, is to create a firewall—a kind of spiritual protection for the flame that carries the heat and the light of our souls.

As sure as night follows day, obstacles will befall you on any worthwhile journey. The willingness to risk everything on behalf of your passion is what makes you an artist.

Keep the faith; keep moving. Remember some brave souls do come back from the dead, as it were. Curator of the photography department at New York's MOMA, John Szarkowski, tells such a story. In the early 1960s, an old man arrived at his office carrying bags full of photographs. It was Andre Kertesz, thought to be dead for thirty years. Not long after his resurrection, he was granted solo exhibitions at MOMA and at the Bibliothéque Nationale in Paris. You can't fail if you don't give up.

BURN-OUT IN A NUTSHELL

> *Those who don't stop to stoke the fire find themselves cold and lonely next to the smoky fireplace.*
>
> *What put out the fire can also relight it, if the embers are stirred and rekindled.*
>
> *Within every dying fire is a spark ready to become a brilliant blaze.*

CAN YOU FEEL THE PHOENIX RISING IN YOU?

Can you sense your wounds healing?

Do you have the strength to go on?

PART III

Realization

[I write] because Indians always tell a story.
The only way to continue is to tell a story and
    that's what Coyote says:
"The only way to continue is to tell a story and
    there is no other way.
Your children will not survive unless you tell
    something about them—
how they were born, how they came to this cer-
    tain place, how they continued."
. . . For my children, for my wife, for my mother
    and my father and my
Grandparents—and then in reverse order so that
    I may have
a good journey on my way back home.
                    —Simon Ortiz, *Winged Words*

Balance of Shadows. Oil on linen by Gregg Chadwick, 2004.

Steel Guitar. Steel sculpture by Karly Stribling, 2003.

CHAPTER 8

Real Work

> *And then I asked myself a lot: what is the real work?*
> *I think it's important, first of all, because it's good to work—*
> *I love work, work and play are one . . . The real work is*
> *what we really do. And what our lives are.*
> *And if we can live the work we have to do, knowing that*
> *we are real, and it's real, and that the world is real,*
> *then it becomes right. And that's the real work:*
> *to make the world as real as it is, and to find*
> *ourselves as real as we are within it.*
>
> —Gary Snyder, *The Real Work*

You've made the journey from inspiration to perspiration. The third stage of the journey reveals the *purpose* of your voyage. In the first stage, you became one with your reverie, made time for your work, and came to know your mentors and muses. In the second stage, you created sacred space, focused deeply on your vision, and learned the dangers of burn-out. On this last stage of the journey, the heat and light of your creative fire illuminates your soul.

Sometimes it seems like a miracle to me—or at least an epiphany—that certain charmed words and images survive the ravages of time so folks like you and I can feel the surge of courage and endurance we need to complete our work and eventually move it out into the world. San Francisco poet and painter Lawrence Ferlinghetti, in an essay for the *San Francisco Chronicle,* agrees: "Such original conceptions of reality are after all why we read poetry or look at art, to throw some light on our own lives and loves, or somehow fathom man's fate, to find clues to the meaning of our still mysterious existence on Earth. We yearn for the epiphany that will reveal all." Legendary painter and art teacher Robert Henri wrote in his ambrosial book *The Art Spirit,* "The object is not to make art but to be in the wonderful state, which makes art inevitable." Igor Stravinsky described this receptivity as "the faculty that helps us pass from the level of conception to the level of realization." The first six stages of the creative journey help to create this "wonderful state"— a reverie of hope and resolve to excel at whatever you attempt. Now you'll learn that the great experiment that is human creativity is a long, meandering road that takes you home again—back to the place where your journey began.

CROSSING THE EQUATOR

On his sea voyage to the Galapagos, Charles Darwin witnessed a mythic ritual that dated back centuries. When the ship crossed the equator, he wrote in his account of the journey, "the sailors were blindfolded, wrapped in a sail filled with water, and then roughly shoved with razor-sharp sticks into a tank of shaving cream." For five years, I pondered this mysterious ritual and especially its relevance to journeys in general. I finally came to the conclusion that the curious ceremony was a kind of initiation rite signifying the transition from the known to the unknown in any journey—a sea voyage, an exploration of new worlds, a venturing forth of ideas and creative visions. These are all variations on the theme of transition or journey. The ancients recognized the significance of these transitions by marking them with proper ceremony.

We all have ritual acts we use to inaugurate new projects—to make the transition from the known to the unknown. We all have our private superstitions, habits, or rites that we hope will positively influence the progress of our work. When I start a new project, I create a little altar on my writing desk by stacking my sacred books, iconic photographs, holy travel souvenirs, and lucky pens there. I call my old writing teachers and writing partners. I wear my father's tattered old sweaters. Chilean novelist Isabelle Allende always begins her novels on the same day of the year (January 8) and always uses the same pen. J. H. Halliday, an expert on the California Gold Rush, begins every day's writing by looking at old engravings of early miners and reading their journals.

Whatever it takes to cross the equator, right?

In the spring of 1985, I interviewed Joseph Campbell for the documentary film *The Hero's Journey*. On the second morning of filming, I saw him slip away into the one quiet corner in the room and found him running his fingers across the leather bindings of a long row of books. As I approached him, he said, "Phil, these twelve books hold some of my fondest memories, as well as some of my best work." When I looked, I saw that they were the twelve volumes on Hinduism, Asian art, and mythology by his mentor, Heinrich Zimmer. Campbell had edited the works.

"Ten years," he said, slowly, "ten years I spent on this work."

Blithely, when I asked him why, he gave an answer that has deeply influenced the way I've looked at the very idea of work ever since.

"His wife asked me to finish them," he said, matter-of-factly. "It was the right thing to do. One day Zimmer was lecturing at Columbia, and the next day he was gone. Dead of pneumonia at forty-four."

So rather than doing his own original work, he took the higher road, helping preserve his teacher's brilliant opus. He did it out of respect and gratitude for the gift Zimmer had given him—the power to think symbolically.

"Zimmer could talk for three hours on the mythology of an *egg*," he laughed. "He taught me that everything has its mythic depths, as Joyce did when he said 'Everything deeply considered is a gateway to the gods.' And he taught me one more lesson—that you teach with the same rigor and passion whether there are three or three hundred students in the auditorium."

When I asked him how he was able to find Zimmer's voice in order to finish the books, his face brightened. "Oh, now this is what I really want to talk about," he said. He then described how, step by step, he had separated all of Zimmer's papers into three piles: his class notes, his own notes from the classes, and the early drafts of each of the unfinished books. Then he closed his eyes and waited until he could feel what he called Zimmer's *presence* in the room. When Zimmer's voice filled Campbell's third ear, as the Sufis call it, he began to write, as much in Zimmer's voice as possible. "When the first reviews came in," he said, "they said that reading these volumes was the next best thing to sitting in on one of Zimmer's legendary lectures."

In earlier times, this would have been called apprenticeship. For many centuries, working with a master was the noble path artists and scholars took before daring to move on to their own work.

I think what impressed me most about Campbell was his discipline. When he was sitting before us on camera, his concentration was unswerving. But whenever we stopped shooting, he seized the moments to swivel around in his armchair, grab his pen, and pick up exactly where he had left off in that day's work. Months later, I came across some photographs of Campbell during his career at Columbia University. In the immortal words of Henry James: "There was the same thing I saw before again." Etched in Campbell's sweat-streamed face was the same fierce resoluteness that allowed him go beyond ordinary effort to the extraordinary. These images, and my memories of our interview, haven given me the courage to recognize profound depths in every kind of work. Having punched a time clock in a steel factory and harvested date trees on a kibbutz, I have a deep and abiding respect for manual labor. But there is also a virtue and power to what typeset designer Eric Gill called "the holy work." This is the real work, the work we were meant to do, the work that makes us *whole*.

In a *Paris Review* interview in 2005, Jack Gilbert alluded to this numinous work when he said about his exacting standards, "There are poems that make you want to do *something else*." This hints at the intensity of his own search for real gold in the lead of his early drafts, and may explain why Gilbert takes an average of ten years to write a book. That mysterious "something else," that leaping of the imagination, those sparks that fly from the word to the heart when read, those colors that vibrate in your spine, those notes that lift your spirit—they are the proof of the real work.

What are you feeling right now, at this moment, at this stage of your work? As the Irish say, How's your heart? How's your fire? How's your stamina? You've come so far: you've achieved your first reverie, scheduled your time, cultivated a healthy relationship with your mentor or muse, set aside a creative space, mastered your focus, and fought the good fight with the dragon of self-doubt. And now here you are with your work begun—maybe even half-complete—and you're wondering if it's good enough. Maybe you're wondering if *you're* good enough. You may be asking yourself why you ever began, why it's been such a long haul. And all along, the *real* issue is whether what you're doing is the *real work*—the work you were meant to do, the work you would do if you knew you only had a year to live, the work you would do if it was the only thing for which you'd be remembered.

We all feel this tremendous, but often inexplicable, inner drive to do only our best work. And there's only one way to get to that work, to the truth of your creative calling. Perhaps

Rilke put it best when he advised an earnest young poet to "Go deeper." The Knoxville sculptor Karly Stribling concurs; "The key," she recently wrote to me, "is to be amazed by the simplest of things—the shadows, the leaves, the blueness of sky. Even the gutter in the street can trigger in me the desire to work. But I have to act, grab the time to draw, sketch, or go to the foundry."

EINSTEIN'S THREE RULES OF WORK

Out of clutter, find simplicity.

From discord, find harmony.

In the middle of difficulty lies opportunity.

Homage to Nancy Oliveri. Wood sculpture by Larry Coleman, 2007.

WHEN IT'S INK

So there is work, and then there is the *real work*. I've spent my life trying to understand the difference. I've done my "hard time"—in a factory, on a kibbutz farm, on construction sites— and I've done *real time*—volunteer coaching, teaching, consulting, and *pro bono* film work. Whenever anyone asks me if there was a moment when I knew what kind of work I *really* wanted to do, a crafty smile comes across my face and a mysterious heat flares in my heart. "Yes," I say, "I remember it because I can still hear it, I can still smell it, I can still feel it in my fingertips. That's why I'm haunted by it."

For me, it happened when I walked into the offices of my hometown newspaper as a young boy. I can still smell the ink and the cold coffee and the stale cigarettes; I can still hear the clatter of typesetting machines, the constant trilling of telephones, and the Tigers' ballgame on WJR. When I arrived for my first night of work as a cub reporter, the crafty old editor, Roger Turner, was huddled over his old typewriter with a cigar stuck in his mouth, actually shouting out his story as he typed it, like Cary Grant in *The Front Page*. "Got your story for me?" he bellowed without looking up. Before I had a chance to answer, he spoke the words that have stayed with me ever since: "*When it's ink, it's real!*" I knew then and there what I wanted to do with the rest of my life. I wanted to be part of that world of whirling-dervish energy, with all its fierce purpose, its laughter, its arguments. Watching the transformation that stories went through between the editor's desk and the layout desk, and then watching them turn into fully designed pages and a full newspaper was astonishing to a sixteen-year-old kid.

Ever since those all-night sessions at the *Dispatch*, I've been fascinated with the path, the process, the journey that is at the heart of all real creative work. I've looked at every book, film, photography assignment, and lecture as a journey, and regarded every journey as a kind of story, a narrative, a drama. Not a day goes by in my writing life that I don't hear that refrain about nothing being real until it's been researched, written, and edited. *When it's ink, it's real!* Looking back, I'm not sure which I loved more: the chance to write and have my own column, or the chance to stay up all night and drive a newspaper truck. It was all way beyond cool; it was life squared, life intensified, life that mattered, life with a

Ahoy! Blow the Glass! Fire Panel Mosaic (detail). Betty Rosen and the staff and visitors to the Museum of Glass, Tacoma, WA. Photograph by Barb White, 2006.

purpose—a life of *real work*. I had my own byline. My heart was on fire.

When in doubt, go back to the beginning. There is a coiled dragon of energy there. Try to remember why you do what you do. When I'm feeling lacerated with self-doubt about my work, I let my mind wander back to that little newspaper office in Wayne. Slowly, as the smell of ink and the sound of clacketing typsetting machines comes back to me, I remember why I believe in the real work. I smile, and my resolve is strengthened.

EXERCISE 18. Five Ways to Do Real Work

Remind yourself why you're doing what you're doing—or ask someone to remind you, as biographer Gerald Nicosia once asked me to do. It helps us return to the original fire.

Be genuinely enthusiastic. Remember it means "to be filled with the gods," which suggests that there is something divine going on in creative work. If we become self-conscious about our enthusiasm or fail to show it, we're likely to become goaded into the cult of the ironic and the jaded.

Be your own fire: The Sufis say there are three ways to experience fire: "See fire; be burnt by fire; be fire." Don't wait for that Guggenheim grant to get started. Let your creative vision ignite you, then burn with your creative fire.

Make it your own. To paraphrase Yogi Berra, "It ain't yours, till it's yours." The real work is *re-creation*—the reworking of your experience, the revisioning of your dreams.

Be aware of what isn't on the page or canvas. The prescient Willa Cather's blazing literary insight applies to all the arts. What's creative isn't apparent to the eye, but felt without being specific. Instead, "It is the inexplicable presence of the thing not named." Go over your work: does it have the presence of something greater than what meets the eye or ear? Is it real?

THE REAL THING

The workplace is full of Fool's Gold. I've known plenty of big-hearted folks who have working-class jobs by day and are volunteers in hospitals. And I've known limo-loads of so-called celebrities who've made millions doing work they secretly hate, with people they despise, repeating themselves, copying others, or debasing their vision. Reflecting on the great range of approaches to work can help you identify the real thing and search the contours of your own capacity to create.

Despite the postmodern palaver that reality is nothing but an illusion, everyone who has honestly attempted to create something from their soul knows the difference between spurious and genuine work. We know it because we live to perform and to create work that has meaning and purpose and life to it.

Ray Bradbury once said that his formula for becoming a prolific writer was really a question: "What do you want more than anything else in the world? Well, then write about it with 'zest and gusto.'" Paul Klee, a favorite painter of mine, had a different experience. In his classic work, *On Painting,* Klee gives one of the most clarion-clear descriptions of the creative process I have ever found:

> *Sometimes I dream of a work of really great breadth, ranging through the whole region of element, object, meaning and style. This, I fear, will remain a dream, but it is a good thing even now to bear the possibility occasionally in mind. Nothing can be rushed. It must grow, it should grow of itself, and if the time ever comes for that work—then so much the better! We must go on seeking! We have found parts, but not the whole.*

Sometimes what's called for is a clean break from the past, a recognition of the creative rust that sometimes forms in the gears of our imagination. Painter Georgia O'Keeffe expressed her own sense of discontent in her autobiography: "One day, seven years ago, I found myself saying to myself I can't live where I want to—I can't go where I want to go—I can't do what I want to do—I can't even say what I want to say . . . I decided I was a very stupid fool not to at least paint as I wanted to." This is a spectacularly honest way to admit to your own failings, while making the decision to break away and follow your own singular voice. To do this demands courage. French architect and author Fernand Pouillon beautifully described this *cri de coeur* in his evocative book, *The Stones of the Abbey,* which follows the life of an orphan who is apprenticed to a stone mason and finally designs and builds the sublime abbey at Le Thoronet, in Provence. Pouillon writes:

> *Creation happens when boldness is released at the very moment that something brilliant is done. Timidity produces nothing of value, and the timid are legion. They think of themselves, of other people, and of what people might say. They wonder if they are sufficiently original or sufficiently with the trend. They do not know what they like. The pusillanimous creator with a critical eye says: "No, that's not enough," or "No, that's too much." That "too much," that "not enough," has to satisfy and flatter and be the soul of the work; it is a great deal to ask of it . . . Courage lies in being oneself, in showing complete independence, in loving what one loves, in discovering the deep roots of one's feelings. A work must not be a copy, one of a group, but unique, sound and untainted, springing from the heart, the intelligence, the sensibility. A real work is truth, direct and honest . . . Never is one's courage courageous enough, never is one's sincerity sincere enough. You have to take the greatest possible risks; even recklessness seems a bit halfhearted. The best works are those*

that are at the limits of real life; they stand out among a thousand others when they prompt the remark: "What courage that must have taken!"

In 1986, I had tea with the humanist psychologist Rollo May at his home in Tiburon, California. That day, he told me that only one thing had saved him in his thirties, when he had a severe mental collapse. "It was beauty, sheer beauty," he told me, his gaze moving over to a bust of Apollo in his den. "I spent two years in Greece just hitchhiking and doing watercolors. Focusing on the beauty of classical Greece and rendering it in my own art somehow saved my life. That's when I decided that the way I could help others was by guiding them to their *real work*."

When I was a young boy growing up in Detroit, my introduction to the world of art by my parents, on weekend visits to the Detroit Institute of Arts, had a similar effect. I particularly recall Diego Rivera's great mural on the nobility of work that had been on display there since 1940. In his autobiography, Rivera describes how, on a trip to Europe in 1913, he became aware of the kind of work he was destined to do. While gazing at the Velasquez paintings at the Prado, he had:

. . . a vision of my vocation to produce true complete pictures of the life of the toiling masses . . . I had reached the Cubist phase of my development . . . and it dawned on me that all this innovation had little to do with real life, I would surrender all the glory and acclaim cubism had brought me for a

*way in art truer to my own feelings . . . I started
on the path one beautifully light afternoon in
1917. Leaving the famous gallery of my dealer,
Leonce Rosenberg, I saw a curbside pushcart
filled with [peaches]. I stood there transfixed, my
eyes absorbing every detail. With unbelievable
force, the texture, forms, and colors of the peaches
seemed to reach out toward me. I rushed back to
my studio and began my experiments that very
day. Nevertheless, the beginning proved painful and tedious. In the process of tearing myself
away from cubism, I met with repeated failures. I
did not give up. It was as if an invisible force was
pushing me onward . . . In human creation there
is something which belongs to humanity at large,
no individual owner has the right to destroy it or
keep it solely for his own enjoyment.*

In 1980, on a hitchhiking trip around the British Isles,
I visited the sculpture studio of Barbara Hepworth in Cornwall. Captivated by her sinuous work, I purchased a copy
of her autobiography and read a passage about work that's
been useful to me ever since. "Working realistically replen-
ishes one's love for life, humanity and the earth," she wrote.
"Working abstractly seems to release one's personality and
sharpen the perceptions, so that in the observation of life,
it is the wholeness or inner intention, which moves one so
profoundly: the components fall into place, the detail is significant of unity."

What is real about your work is real about your inward life. The haunted storyteller Spaulding Gray used to talk into a tape recorder to find his real voice for each new work. Psychologist Viktor Frankl often lectured about how those who survived the death camps had a reason and a purpose to live, concluding, "If you have a *why* you can survive any *how*." When the Irish upstart James Joyce was in his early twenties, he kept a notebook in which he recorded seventy "epiphanies," a word he rescued from the musty books of theology. These epiphanies became the seed moments for all his short stories, poems, plays, and novels.

There is another force that pulls us forward through the narrow channel between the rocks of doubt and cynicism, and that is sheer beauty. The 14th-century Arabic poet Hafiz once wrote, "God courts us with the beauty in this world." That single line is worth any number of Ph.D. dissertations on art. In poetic terms, it brings to the forefront the magnetic power of beauty to attract us with the force of the stars in the heavens. I've heard it from hundreds of creative people over the years: "There is something in my work pulling me forward." "It's bulldogging me; it won't let go." What they're feeling is the gravitational force of destiny. "I don't take the photograph," insisted Cartier-Bresson, "it takes me."

EXERCISE 19. Six Ways to Get to Work

Surprise yourself. Take a risk: write in a new genre, use an entirely new spectrum of colors, sing in a different key. Dare to be yourself.

When in doubt, do it. Keep a notebook or sketchbook handy. Write, paint, compose, sculpt, make a blueprint. There will always be a voice to keep you back, distract you, criticize you. Ignore it; move on.

Strangify your work. Teachers like John Gardner say there's no art without strangeness. Defamiliarize yourself. Get your "freak" on, as Jim Carrey says. Take a walk on the wild side by writing in the voice of somebody peculiar to you.

Bonify your work. Make it good; make it beautiful. Take it down, deep, into your soul.

Call your work holy. Dare to stand up for the spirit that enlivens real work.

One for the Man, One for Me. It's the old refrain from the streets of Detroit. It means do what it takes to pay the bills, but every day, in every way, . do something, make something for your soul. Start today—and it can't be for money or fame.

I'm what used to be called in Shakespeare's time a "carrytale," someone who bears a tale from town to town. I collect stories of how artists and writers work the way other people collect butterflies, stamps, or coins. I get a kick out of knowing that the Beach Boys' Brian Wilson had eight tons of sand poured into his home to remind him of the California beaches. It's wonderful to know that David Bowie clips headlines out of newspapers, scrambles them in his computer, and makes songs out of the garbled words. Jack Kerouac wrote on the bathroom floor. Glass artist Dale Chihuly works in the bathtub. Hank Williams and Gertrude Stein both wrote in their cars. Rilke wrote seventy-two poems about animals at the Paris zoo. What do these stories have in common? They exemplify the uncommon courage it takes to get to the bottom of your life, the compulsion to get words or images out of your soul that will somehow redeem your life. They are an affirmation of the creative life itself.

EXERCISE 20. Five Ways to Stay True to the Real Work Focused

Make it new, as Ezra Pound said, or, to quote Groucho Marx, "Better nouveau than never." Now is the time to go as far as you can with your talent. And that always feels new. The surefire proof is when you look it over and you wonder, "Who did that?"

For your next project, try something you can't possibly do. Henry Moore once told Donald Hall this was the one and only secret task for an artist.

Take notes. For two hours, take notes on a movie that you've rented or viewed in a theater; use a light pen so you don't make yourself too self-conscious. What would you do differently? Now write a ten-minute movie.

Just listen. For the length of one conversation, remember the American Indian saying, "Listen or your words will make you deaf." Now record it like a found poem, make a collage of the experience and see if it doesn't surprise you.

Look for the wolf in your work, the primal force. That's the sure sign it's the real thing.

A LIFE LIVED

For my money, Gerald Nicosia's biography of Jack Kerouac, *Memory Babe,* is one of the most illuminating books of its kind in our time. Nicosia has lived and breathed not only Kerouac's life, but the spiritual dimensions of the Beat movement and other vital stories of our time. Recently, we spoke about the creative role of writing biographies, which the Jesuits

Jack Kerouac biographer Gerald Nicosia with Jan Kerouac. Photograph courtesy of Gerald Nicosia.

taught me is one of the most incisive psychological and spiritual practices.

> The poet Sharon Doubiago once said it is unethical to attempt to write the life of someone you don't like. I would go even further. I would say it is unethical to write the biography of someone whose life you cannot, in some way, imagine yourself living or having lived. There is a strong element of method acting in all great biographies. One needs to identify, or at least be able to identify with, one's subject. Plain and simple. By that, I do not mean that one should write a biography uncritically, or even without at times heavy censure of one's subject (if he or she deserves it)—but all criticism should be just as one criticizes oneself: with a good measure of love. By the same token, the biographer must be as honest in writing about his/her subject as one is honest in considering one's own self—in the privacy of one's thoughts. Neither mercenary interests nor pressure from opinionated outsiders should figure into the biographical record, any more than one would factor them into one's private view of oneself. But to write such a biography takes great courage—even as living a heroic, nonconformist life takes great courage.

Create a biographical work. Paint a portrait. Compose a song. The work must be of someone you admire or believe has a story that's gone untold and can be instructive. The contours of that story will illuminate your own.

Create an autobiography. However long or short, illustrated or not, sketched, filmed, sung, an exercise in autobiography is worth any number of academic degrees. Ask yourself, as the Comanche painter Rance Hood once did, "Let us see, is this real, this life I am living?" If so, write about how you can make it even more real, more true.

When he was secretary to the sculptor Auguste Rodin, the German poet Rainer Rilke often heard him cite the old medieval craft-saying: "Work . . . and you will know the grace of great things." What a marvelous expression! It evokes the notion of creativity as the capacity to imagine and make something not only new and original, but something that transcends commercial or utilitarian concerns. It reminds us of the reality of the soul's strange necessity to respond when we are moved. There is something that burns like a branding in the soul of creative people. Something happens and *we must respond*—in word, paint, or stone. This is the marrow in the bone, the stuff of life, the creative urge, the compulsion that longs to be what John Dewey called the *impulsion*—the urge toward completion. What a word. It's the exact opposite of "compulsion," which is usually a pejorative when used to describe creative characters. It is one of the most fascinating elements of human life, and one that lies at the heart of my own. That is why I believe in each of us making our own Museum of the Imagination, filled with collections of stories and images that inspire us to keep going with our work.

We all draw inspiration from the stories of the world's creators and seekers who came before us—some famous, others notorious. I can't forget Vermeer's luminous painting *Woman in Blue Reading a Letter*. Seamus Heaney describes how he dug into the translation of *Beowulf* by visiting his Northern Ireland neighbors to infuse the work with the most authentic Anglo-Saxon words possible. Max Perkins compressed Thomas Wolfe's trunk full of manuscript pages into *The Town and the City*.

Tony Bennett describes his work habits as "so meditative, you could paint for four hours and it seems like four minutes—the concentration that takes over you. They say, Life is short, but art is long." Yoko Ono recollects the recording of "Imagine" with her husband, John Lennon: "It was all of us around who came together. We made a ring around the world together." All these stories, and thousands more, rev my engine; they get my adrenaline rushing; they stoke my fire.

E. L. Doctorow wrote of Arthur Miller, "There is always a day of reckoning: it arrives at that point in a man's life when truth bursts through his self-delusion and he is overwhelmed." I think the reckoning has to do with whether our work is going to be creative or Creative. Knowing others have been illuminated by the passion for the real work reaffirms my hope for the human race. It has to do with the courage to move from inspiration through perspiration to realization—no matter how surreal the idea may seem at the time.

Where will your imagination take you if you unleash it? What is your image for work? What is your ideal? What is most real for you? What is holy? When a New York reporter asked Matisse if he believed in God, *le maitre* replied: "Only when I work." What is truly marvelous about the creative urge is that it allows you to pursue something that you really love, to lead a life of surprises, to follow the sparks that lead you to the soulful life. This affirmation of life is the ultimate description of the real work that creates a work of art. Only then will your work connect to the larger web of work that connects us all.

REAL WORK IN A NUTSHELL

The real work is what you were meant to do,
> *not to think about, not to speculate on,*
> *not to wonder about, but to do,*
> *to make yourself*
> *a new world.*

HAVE YOU MADE THE REAL TURN IN YOUR WORK?

Does this work finally reveal your secret self?

Does your work throw off sparks?

Cooling Off. Lakeside dock, Lithuania. Photograph by Phil Cousineau, 1996.

CHAPTER 9:

Cool Fire

The real artists' work is a surprise to himself.

—Robert Henri, *The Art Spirit*

The eighth stage of the creative journey is the cool fire, or cooling-down period. After the hot streak of inspiration allows you to be productive, to actually do the work—maybe after talking it to death—the cool fire lets you assimilate your vision before releasing it into the world. Cooling down also gives you a chance to reflect on how the work fits into your career, maybe even your everyday life.

Not everyone stops to smell the ink or the paint. There are tectonic forces pressuring us to be more prolific than reflective. I once visited my publisher's offices the week one of my books hit several bestseller lists. By sheer chance, I bumped into the publisher himself and was delighted when he took my hand and vigorously shook it to congratulate me. "Good going, Cousineau," he said. "We need more *product* like that! We need to move more units like yours!" Stunned, I left the office feeling as if I'd just gotten a slap in the face. All my illusions about creating a work of art went flying—or flopping—out the window. It was a wake-up call to the cold hard reality of the publishing world.

Our culture is permeated by a "hustle factor" that tags anyone who slows down as not being ambitious or successful—as falling fatally behind. Still, we all have a choice at this stage. We can succumb to the hustle factor—churning out work like Pez dispensers—or we can slow down after the completion of each project and "take five," as jazz musicians say. The truth is that we're not all Isaac Asimov, who published 506 books in his lifetime and wondered why others couldn't keep up with him. For the rest of us mere mortals, cooling down is a smart move, because it lets us take one last look at our work—or even our lives—before signing off on the canvas or the galleys. Sometimes, the cool fire lasts a few hours, sometimes many years.

In 1995, I was fortunate to have the documentary film *Ecological Design* I'd written accepted at the Sundance Film Festival. To premier a film at Sundance was an independent filmmaker's dream. The day after our screening, I was chatting with Betty Rosen-Ziff, a music-rights agent for the movie studios, and legendary record producer Don Was, who was screening *I Just Wasn't Made for These Times,* his film about

Brian Wilson, the troubled genius of the Beach Boys. Incredibly, Don invited us to the invitation-only celebration for his "revisionist documentary," casually mentioning that Wilson had promised to attend and maybe even perform a few songs. When Wilson appeared at the party, he shuffled into the room and headed straight for the security of a gleaming black baby-grand piano. Spectral and shy, without lifting his eyes off the keyboard, he played the first few notes of "God Only Knows"—one of the sweetest anthems to young love ever written.

A hush fell over the crowded room of film buffs as Brian segued into "Do It Again," then "Good Vibrations." As I watched him, an odd image came to me.

This is Lazarus coming back from the dead, I thought. Wilson had fought corrosive depression for many years, and now he was singing for his life. After the impromptu performance, the buzz around the room was about a legendary

Brian Wilson at the 1995 Sundance Festival. Photograph by Paula Sartorius.

lost album called *Smile* that Wilson had begun recording in 1968. Rumor had it that he'd never completely abandoned the album. After the festival, I watched and waited for its release. After hearing him play again, I was convinced Wilson wasn't stuck; he was just *brooding*—holding the project in the cool fire, giving it life. By the time I read in *Rolling Stone* that Wilson was planning to premier *Smile* at the Royal Albert Hall, it was early in 2004, almost a decade after I had heard Wilson sing at Sundance. In late 2005, when the shy artist appeared on *The Charlie Rose Show*, he looked like a modest old blues man—cool on top, with the fire down below. When Rose asked him why he'd waited so long to complete the album, Wilson said simply, "The world wasn't ready for it."

When I heard this, I laughed; I felt vindicated for all the times I had taken my time with my own works to "get it right." I wasn't alone after all in wanting to simmer, to hold my most personal projects in the cool fire.

Some works fly from the pen or the brush; others need to gestate. But why? I've tried to answer that question all my life. Doctorow provides a partial answer in his book of literary essays, *Creationists*, where he tells us that the creative act "is never entirely under your control. It cannot be a matter of solely willed expression." Czeslaw Milosz sums it up even more succinctly: "The secret of all art is distance." Why? I believe it's because we need to be sure of what we're looking at, of what we're *feeling*, in our heart of hearts. What was so intimately close to us at the beginning of our project, now, at the end, may feel foreign. Often, we wonder who or what created the work that has our name on it.

COOLING DOWN

There are as many reasons to let a finished work cool down as there are to brood on one that's just begun. It's impossible to say which is harder—to start or to finish. The French poet Paul Valéry once said that a work of art is never really done; it's just abandoned. Arshile Gorky, the Russian painter, admitted that he never really finished his paintings. He just started working on another canvas—sometimes fifteen at a time—until a cold deadline forced him to let them go.

Ideally, your imagination is to your work as the bellows is to the fire—a means for breathing life into the flames. But that breath can take many forms. The spark that ignited a work can also set off a conflagration that may incinerate it later on. Anton Chekhov called for "the cold eye"—the cool perspective that leads to his ideal of concision, which he called "the sister of talent." Hemingway championed a cold editing scalpel so a writer could "kill his darlings," edit out his clever work and leave only the true. Contemporary painter Gregg Chadwick advocates a "cool down" period, similar to the period after a physical workout where you allow your muscles to relax. Only in that cooler time can you make the tough decisions about what to keep and what to discard. Annie Leibovitz admits many of her unforgettable photographs happened after all the meticulous planning, when her subjects were relaxing—or had dropped their guard.

As an artist, you must be self-critical; you must be able to take constructive criticism. You must be cool-hearted, as opposed to cold-hearted. Cultivating the cool fire tempers your ecstasy, which, by definition, is impossible to control but indispensable for releasing your natural genius. And here's the most slippery point of all to convey: Cooling your ardor lets you move into "overtime"; it gives you a last chance to recognize the "otherness" that the *real work* takes on.

If you allow yourself some cool fire, some time to brood over your art—even though the world wants you to quickly move on to the next work—you'll discover qualities and values and *presences* in your art that you might not see if you rush into publication or release. Or you may learn that sitting on the work a little longer can ensure its ethical dimensions.

Nobody I know stoked this cool fire better than Gary Rhine, my film partner and one of my closest friends for nearly twenty years. When Rhino, as everyone called him, was working on his film *Wiping the Tears of Seven Generations,* he called me for help editing the first cut. The film, named for a revered Indian grieving ceremony, was intended to tell the story of the long journey from Custer's Last Stand to Wounded Knee from the Native American perspective.

The film told a powerful story about a 200-year-old wound that was being healed by collectively reliving it—400 men, women, and children riding in the snow for two weeks if fifty-below-zero weather to "wipe away the tears." Rhino was committed to portraying the Indian point of view, even to the extent of submitting every script page and every illustration to the elders of every tribe he filmed and respectfully asking for their blessing. The net result was to "cool down" the filming—sometimes for days, sometimes weeks or months. That extra time allowed the film to breathe, to take on a patina of authenticity and the gleam of dignity because we had sought out the blessing of the elders.

"Coolness" became a kind of code work for us—a reference to getting it right and *making it real*. In the film world, where everything is "hot"—as in accelerated, over-amped, trendy—coolness can be a much-needed antidote to the steamroller approach that drives so much modern filmmaking. I've come to believe that this "cooling-down" period isn't a luxury in the creative process; it's an imperative. It helps you avoid releasing shoddy work; it gives you the chance to move on gracefully to the last phase of the project. Sometimes it lets you see your creation—or yourself—in a completely new light. At other times, it gives you a chance to revisit the work and get it right the second time around. Walt Whitman continually revised his poems, out of love rather than perfectionism. Renoir revisited his own paintings in the Louvre, paint and paintbrush in hand, to give them a little touch up. Feature filmmakers like Terrence Malick or Ridley Scott often brood for years over the way the studios released incomplete versions of their movies before releasing their "director's cut."

EXERCISE 22. Five Ways to Cool Down

Take time to brood. Before delivering your manuscript, canvas, or recording, *sit on it*. Take another look at it in the morning. Let it simmer; let it breathe. Let it sit in your soul for a while, as Abigail Doggett Bordeaux did with her memories of a life-changing pilgrimage before finally making her

The Seven Pilgrimage Chapels. Clay sculptures by Abigail Doggett
Bordeaux, 2006.

seven clay sculptures, which recaptured the stages
of her sacred journey.

Send your work to an elder. Find an expert in your
field. Take a chance. Ask for feedback. Be humble.
Let them cool your ardor. If it's the real fire, it
will return.

Reflect honestly on the work. Ask yourself if you took
enough creative risks. Find a first page, an early sketch,
an original recording. Compare. If you're bored with
the work now, you didn't push yourself hard enough.
What can you do to startle yourself? Ask yourself if
the work measures up to your original vision. If so,
are you happy with it? If not, can you live with it?

Celebrate the work. Throw a party. Loosen up.
Don't take it so seriously. Think of Rousseau reading his *Confessions* to friends all night long before
delivering it. Or Van Morrison singing songs from
Astral Weeks to strangers at an L.A. party before
recording it.

Consider a sideways move. Joni Mitchell recounts how boxed-in she felt by the music business and how she didn't want to be a "human jukebox." So she began to paint, a move that redoubled her creativity. Try a new medium. Test your vision.

Laugh about it. Tape up some cartoons around your studio, such as the *New Yorker* one called "James Joyce's Refrigerator Notes." The caption reads: (1) Call bank (2) Dry Cleaner (3) Forge in the smithy of my soul the uncreated conscience of my race (4) Call mom.

REFLECTION IN COOL TRANQUILITY

In the summer of 1919, in the foothills of Yosemite Valley, Ansel Adams looked up and saw something so sublime that it radically changed his life. He watched as a supernal light shone across the valley, illuminating the inner life of every single tree and blade of grass. Time stopped; space seemed suspended. He found himself in a kind of limbo and felt an uncanny sense of the oneness of all creation. Adams was so thoroughly transformed by that radiant light that he spent the rest of his life trying to recapture its beauty and intensity. The young photographer's ecstatic experience is iconic. His story symbolizes for many artists the moment of aesthetic arrest—the unifying experience that becomes the gold standard for the rest of your life. In Adams' case, the epiphany precipitated a dark-room discipline that historians of photography debate to this day. Rather than settle for "first print, best print," the print that's first exhibited or published,

Adams reprinted even his most famous photographs over and over.

Why? What was he seeking? One possibility lies in the fascinating practice that Adams called "pre-visualization." Adams' son Michael tells me that his father spent a great deal of time before leaving for shoots in Yosemite or the Sierras trying to imagine what he was going to see. He learned how to anticipate the kind of light he might encounter and which cameras to use—which is another way of saying that he learned how powerful reverie was in his artistic process. Some of these active-imagination exercises were so vivid that the final result—the prints he made in his Carmel darkroom—did not fulfill the expectations of his own creative power. Rather than settle for less, no matter how acclaimed the photographs or how harsh the criticism, Adams returned again and again to the darkroom, knowing it's wiser to satisfy your soul than your ego.

Confidence in your creative capacity comes from knowing you are prepared, which means knowing your lines as an actor, knowing the available ingredients in the kitchen, or knowing the way light falls on the pine trees and then capturing it. But it also comes from learning to trust your own maturing judgment as you become more adept in your work. It's insufficient to dismiss Adams as a perfectionist. He had a glimpse of timeless beauty and he wanted another taste of it. His reprinting of even his most famous photographs was a "cool fire" exercise that encouraged him to be humble and seek, not just the light, but *the dark thread* that wends its way through all sublime art. It's the grounding force.

The creative moment is one of delight and astonishment. As artists, that's what we live for. That's why we love magicians, jokes, plays and movies, sports, some birthday parties, and whatever lurks just around the corner. But sometimes the revelation comes after that initial moment of creation. Sometimes it comes in your moments of reflection—of cooling down. That's when it comes to you: the *real* thing—the art—is always a surprise, like the timeless photo I took of Casa Grande.

There is a breathtaking stained-glass window by Marc Chagall in the Art Institute of Chicago. On the description plate next to it, the great Russian artist is quoted as saying, "I like a life of surprises." I think that statement cuts to the heart

The Reenchantment of Ruins, **Casa Grande, Arizona. Infrared photograph by Phil Cousineau, 2006.**

of the creative process. Outsiders tend to think that artists know exactly what they're going to paint, writers what they're going to write, and so on. But when cornered, most will confide that the real thrill is knowing that you don't know—and more—knowing that you're *about to know*. You know that there's a tremendous surprise in store if you keep going, but sometimes, you need to "cool down" to reveal it—to reveal the real promise of your work.

In a 1998 interview, legendary songwriter and keyboardist Mike Pinder told me why, in 1978, he left rock and roll "to come back to the tribe." His story illustrates how powerful the cool fire can be. "The seeds of my philosophy," Pinder told me, "are there at the family piano playing notes and feeling the speed of vibrations and strings. If you understand an octave above and an octave below you understand the entire universe. It's that simple." But after a meteoric career in which he sold over a hundred million records with the Moody Blues, he found himself one night in Las Vegas rooted to the dressing room, unable to move and completely indifferent to performing. He recalls that it was as if his total being—body, mind, and spirit—were all rebelling, and he refused to go on stage.

So he quit.

Instead, he read, traveled, and researched myths, legends, and fables. In essence, he cooled down for the next seven years, until he found what he laughingly calls his "real work in the real world." This has included solo recordings that are poetic reveries about his life-long belief in the journey toward higher consciousness, and two albums of myths, poetry, and music for children. "This is the real Hall of Fame," Pinder told me, claiming that the response to these works has been far more gratifying than the applause of crowds during his days as a rock star. He believes that the hope for the future lies in working with the innate creativity of children, who can directly experience the great attributes of the human spirit through myths and music—although he fears that gift can easily be lost in a world drowning in materialism. Though traumatic at the time, Pinder is certain that his sudden change of life—his commitment to cool down—allowed him the time and the freedom to reinvent himself and gave him the opportunity to use his creative gifts in a new way. "It's so simple it evades," he told me. "All you have to do is trade the unreal for the real." Now that's how you cool down and rekindle your fire.

Creative souls throughout the ages have gestated ideas for years and sometimes decades. For some, idea and execution go side by side. Bob Dylan wrote "I and I" in five minutes. Yet Leonard Cohen took two years to write "Hallelujah." In the final sublime scenes of *Immortal Beloved,* the film about the life of Beethoven, the deaf and dying composer is on stage in Vienna as the orchestra begins his Ninth Symphony, the famous "Ode to Joy." Tragically, as we know, Beethoven couldn't hear his own divine music. But he could feel the vibrations coming up through the floorboards. In the film, the movement triggers a memory. The scene cuts to the young Beethoven lying on his back looking up at the stars twinkling above, listening to what turn out to be the opening notes from the "Ode to Joy." Sometimes it takes a lifetime for a creative work to "cool down."

Paul Gauguin had three simple rules for creating his own works: Dream on it; simplify it; rectify it. Think of those rules as you do this next series of cooling down exercises.

EXERCISE 23. Five Cooling-Down Techniques

Sleep on it. Visualize your completed work as you're falling asleep.

Often, the confirmation about it comes from the shadowland of dreams. Remember how the project began and how it's been realized. Dream on it.

Keep it simple. Simplifying at this stage doesn't mean dumbing down. It refers to letting go of all the unreasonable expectations and learning to live with the now very real work of art you have in your hands. Don't think of results right now. As James Baldwin said, the word "success" shouldn't be in any artist's vocabulary. Excellence, yes; success, no.

Rectify and edify. Go over the work one last time, casually, easily, gratefully. Take your time fixing any mistakes, improving it one last time. And then remember the old French maxim, "A work is never done; it's only abandoned."

Work, Don't Think, Rest. With the blessings of the great Ray Bradbury, you can let it—and you—rest.

Lean back and enjoy. Twenty-five centuries ago, Lao Tzu said, "Do the work, then step back. The only path to serenity." In other words, cool it.

THE BIRTH OF COOL

In one of my all-time favorite movies about the artist's life, *The Horse's Mouth*, the redoubtable Alec Guinness plays an eccentric, obsessed, bloviating, lovable crank of a painter named Gully Jimson, who lives on a houseboat in London. Throughout the movie, a young wannabe artist follows him around, asking him to pass on his wisdom. Finally, the exasperated Guinness says, "You have to know when you've failed and when you've succeeded . . . Everybody wants to be an artist once—and then they grow up!"

In those moments when you reread or review your work, you have to look in the mirror and see if you can change something in yourself or in your work that can keep the real work moving forward. One of the most gripping examples of this that I've discovered is related in Bob Dylan's *Chronicles*. Dylan tells of a party in Alan Lomax's loft in Greenwich Village where he heard Mike Seeger, of the New Lost City Ramblers, sing. Dylan describes Seeger as radiating a kind of "telepathy" as he played the old folk songs. The blistering authenticity of the performance shifted something essential in Dylan's soul. "Nobody could just learn this stuff," Dylan confesses, "and it dawned on me that I might have to change my inner thought patterns . . . that I would have to start believing in possibilities that I couldn't have allowed before, that I had been closing my creativity down to a very narrow, controllable scale . . . that things had become too familiar and I might have to disorient myself."

The creative whiplash that Dylan felt came from the mysterious force of inspiration being transmuted into the vision of seeing his own *possible self* in another human being and wanting to replicate the *courage* that compelled someone else to become themselves. There and then, Dylan recounts, he decided to write his own songs, "a startling thought" that was frightening because he knew it would open the door into an unknown world.

That's the birth of cool, the constant rebirth of art in the fires of ecstasy tempered by cool control.

And now ask yourself these key questions as you review your work of art, whatever shape it has taken. *Does it rise?* This was Flannery O'Connor's test for the transcendent in art. *Does it inspire a cleansing awe?* as David Mamet believes

Le Penseur (The Thinker).
Marble sculpture by Auguste
Rodin, Rodin's House, Paris,
France. Photograph by Phil
Cousineau, 1997.

distinguishes between art and entertainment. *Does it haunt?* This is my own standard for work I release into the world. It must make my own heart race, if it is to move anyone else.

COOL FIRE IN A NUTSHELL

> *Creativity is fiery feeling plus cool observation.*
> *If it didn't surprise you it won't surprise your*
>   *audience.*
> *Take time to brood then trust the new life that*
>   *hatches in you.*

HAVE YOU COOLED DOWN
LONG ENOUGH?

Can you feel the truth about your work?

Do you stand by it—and can you let it go?

Reconciliation. Oil painting by Leigh Ferguson, 2005.

CHAPTER 10:

Passing the Torch

I begin to see what I had in mind.

—Virginia Woolf

There may be self-expression in solitude, but there is not art without connection to the community. My mythic image for this is the passing of the torch. In pre-classical times, the first competitions at Olympia were footraces to the fire-lit altar of Zeus where the winner was awarded a torch. Today, the passing of the torch signifies the movement of anything significant from one generation to the next. I see it as the ninth stage of the creative journey, the object of your long voyage of realization. The fire will flicker out unless it heats new hands; the project is incomplete unless passed on to ignite other spirits,

Prometheus Creating a Human Being and *Prometheus Giving the Gift of Fire.*
Medieval engravings.

which in turn sparks a whole new round of creativity in both the individual and the group.

A MODERN PARABLE

In the summer of 1978, in the gently rolling hills north of Turin, Italy, eleven friends gathered around a flickering fire. One of them was a twenty-eight-year-old writer, artist, and gentle visionary named Oberto Airaudi. He had tried his hand in the business world, but had soon wearied of its spiritually stultifying atmosphere. Now he was considering a different kind of future. Oberto had a dream of constructing a series of sacred underground temples the likes of which had not been built for 1000 years or more—The Temples of Humankind. And he had the willpower to turn it into reality.

But first, he needed a sign. It came in the form of a mighty shooting star, a rare event in that part of the continent. Oberto interpreted this as a positive sign, and considered this a good moment to begin digging a tunnel into the mountain, toward the heart of the earth. Everything in the temple, he vowed, would be created by hand, in a job taking an inconceivable amount of time and willpower.

Shortly after the meeting around the fire, Oberto and two others began digging with simple picks, shovels, buckets, chisels, and hammers. Several others joined them that night, and more the next night. Soon groups of four were digging shafts and tunnels in four-hour shifts to help fulfill Oberto's vision of the temples. There gradually developed around the project a self-sustaining community of artists, artisans, farmers, teachers, architects, and builders. Over the next two decades, this group worked at the temple site, which Oberto named Damanhur, after an ancient city in Egypt renowned for its magicians and mystical architecture.

By 2005, the seven subterranean temples had grown into a mind-boggling mix of the Grail Castle, the ancient Minoan labyrinth, Chartres Cathedral, and Biosphere 2—a mosaic of stained-glass splendor, mythic murals, secret passageways, magic mirrors, and meditation halls. Together, they represent the collective creative memory of the human race. They are not a commercial enterprise, but stand as a *gift* from the community of artisans to the world.

In 2005, I interviewed Oberto—now known as Falco—for the documentary film *City 21* on the future of urban life. Damanhur is a place, he told me, where every form of artmaking is exalted. Since the beginning everyone has been regarded as a natural born artist with a divine spark and is encouraged to live accordingly, by which he meant collectively, for the common good. "Whatever myth is at the origin of a culture, if nourished, becomes reality. That means, at Damanhur, we have the Grail." Esperides Ananas, the communications director, added, "I think this is the most advanced experiment in the world, with a new social, economic, and artistic way of living. We believe we can be a great creative model not by following in other's footsteps in the arts but being creative first of all in our life. The idea is that the gift of each one of our artists can be enhanced if they work together, by the sum of their uniqueness. Damanhur's job is to show pathways so people know they can do more than they think they can."

In my mind, the astonishing beauty of the temples is directly linked to this archetypal notion of the gift and its role in demystifying the artist and the creative process while emphasizing community. Countless old stories tell us that wisdom does not come easily. A sacrifice is required; a gift is demanded. The word "gift" derives from *ghebh,* an Indo-European word that means both "to give" and "to receive," as well as "duty" and "provender," a noble old word for food. Giving a gift is thus a complex transaction that keeps communities intact. Ansel Adams wrote in 1937 that art "is both the taking and the giving of beauty." The creative gift is thus the heart of communal life. It is a constant message that is constantly forgotten.

The gift of creativity binds people together because its genuine generosity allows us to transcend our selfishness and consider the welfare of the community. It is not until you learn the joy of giving gifts that you cross the threshold into adulthood. By extension, it's not until you learn that your talent, your creativity, is a gift that you complete on the final stage of the creative journey—and ensure that your creativity keeps moving. As actor Jack Lemmon used to say, "send the elevator back down!" Encourage those still on the ground floor.

EXERCISE 24. Five Ways to Pass the Torch

Tell the story of the actual making of your work to young people. This keeps the gift moving, as Native Americans say it must.

Be kind to your rivals. Fellow writers, filmmakers, painters, singers, poets, dancers—they are also enduring a great struggle.

Volunteer. Spend time in a nursing home. Listen to their stories. Tell others.

Send a gift you have made to someone in a hospital, or to a soldier, a prisoner, a student.

Be a lamp, not a fire extinguisher. Offer to mentor somebody in your field. Be open about the help you've received. If you allow your fire to light somebody else's torch, your fire will never go out.

A CAUTIONARY TALE

In 1952, Chilean poet and diplomat Pablo Neruda was asked to read a poem at a political rally in the coal-mining district of Lota. When his name was announced, 10,000 miners removed their coal-blackened helmets and bent their heads because, he wrote in his *Memoirs,* "poetry itself was about to speak." The pungent odors of coal and briny sea air stung his nose and eyes as he gazed out over the ocean and the dark coal tunnels that stretched for miles. When he began to recite his work, he heard "a ground swell impossible to describe, a huge soundless wave, a black foam of quiet reverence," and was astonished to see miners mouthing the words of his poem along with him.

This story embodies for me the cyclical nature of inspiration, which is an active, not a passive, phenomenon. The poet is inspired, high in his bow-of-a-ship-like writing room, overlooking the pounding sea. He writes; the poems are published; the works learned by heart. He appears in a hellhole of a mine that other celebrated figures wouldn't even think of visiting. Years later, thousands read his version of what happened in his memoirs. Some people read the story as entertainment and quickly forget it. But others, like me, can't get the image out of their minds and feel obligated to pass it on. This slight story holds one of the keys to the creative life—the uncanny ability to move the spirit that stirred your heart into someone else's heart. It's the secret power of inspiration, the power to help us breathe together. It's the passing of the torch.

What exactly is being passed on here? The cult of genius? The brotherhood of poets? Or something more?

Jacob Bronowski offers a clue in *The Visionary Eye:* "It is not the thing done or made that is beautiful, but the doing," he writes. "If we appreciate the thing, it is because we relive the heady freedom of making it." And this is what happens on this final stage of the creative journey—we pass on the "heady freedom" of the creative act.

EXERCISE 25. Three Ways to Stay Stoked

Remember we are all dependent on one another, as Leigh Ferguson says about her painting, *Reconciliation*. "We are spiritually symbiotic and all of us are trying to keep our souls intact." This advice can help you prepare for your next work.

Remember to recognize the fire in others. "I still see the spark in you," whispers a serene corporal to a cynical sergeant in Terrence Malick's *The Thin Red Line*. If you see such a spark in others, you will simultaneously feel the heat in yourself.

Remember da Vinci's last notebook entry: "I shall go on." Will you press on, regardless? What will you write in yours tonight? Tomorrow?

In 1971, a Dutch painter and art teacher, Geoff Barden, made the arduous journey into the Australian Outback to visit an aborigine settlement. One day, he discovered an old man drawing in the dirt. Barden encouraged him to attempt something more permanent and offered him art material. Encouraged, the man created a traditional painting on the wall of the school. "Suddenly," Barden later recalled in the film *Mr. Pattern*, "the universe was being created before my very eyes, mind maps [aerial views] of their sacred lands."

Another aborigine artist said, "Without painting, I would just be another lost soul."

One of the most creative souls I've ever met was an old Negro League ballplayer named Joseph Charles who lived a few blocks from me in Berkeley, California, in the early 1980s. For thirty years, he was out on his front porch wearing a white glove and waving to passing traffic, calling out, "Keep smiling!" and "Have a good day!" He was called "The Happiness Man," and when asked why he did it he simply said that life had treated him "real good" and he wanted to "pass on those feelings."

To me, Mr. Charles was creative in the original sense of the word, he made something—*happiness*—out of nothing. That is what artists do; they make something happen, they make something real, something the world's never (or rarely) seen before. The great truths about creative life turn out to be half-truths in search of their other half. I believe we become more real every time we *realize* ourselves, our destiny, our gifts, and our talents. And in this there is great joy. In this sense, our completed works—our paintings, our albums, our books, our songs, our sculptures—are signs to ourselves and others that we did not cower when asked to take a risk, did not shy away from the struggle, dug deep and played hard.

Perhaps that's what Emily Dickinson meant when she wrote those mysterious words: "My business is circumference." Your business as an artist, your purpose, is not only to begin and to work, but to complete, to come full circle. That's where the satisfaction is. There is power in completion, but also a sense of relief. There's tremendous satisfaction in realizing that you've completed something—when you literally *realize* what's in your heart of hearts, when you complete the long journey to the heart of the work that defines you. Only then can your creative spark light the torch in the hearts of others.

Everything is a circle. The sky, a ball, the circuit of our lives—everything moves a-round. Your task is to set your course and carry on—though you may feel fear, may lose sight of the horizon—until your vision is one with the fire lit in your heart by the torch of inspiration carried by so many others before you.

Now you can say you responded to the challenge of the old Dublin Triad: *This was it. This was the thing. This was the thing you were up against.* And you made something out of it. Soon, you will feel the fire in your heart again. Soon, you will seek a creative adventure of an even fuller fire.

PASSING THE TORCH IN A NUTSHELL

Creativity is a responsibility to express and to pass on.

Celebrate the joy of completing your creative journey.

Take time to make a vow to pass on your gift.

HOW STRONG IS YOUR HEART NOW?

Have you dreamed of a new work?

Can you carry the fire?

The Long Journey Home, seventeenth-century engraving.

Epilog

*Old as I am, there's a great deal more in my head
than I can write down here. I did my best to give
an accurate account of the people I knew, so that we'd
be remembered when we had moved on to eternity.
People will yet walk above our heads; it could even
happen that they'd walk into the graveyard where I'll
be lying, but people like us will never again be there.
We'll be stretched out quietly—
and the old world will have vanished . . .
May God grant that blessing and may He grant it,
too, to those who have read these lines!*

—Meig Sayers, *Blasket Islands*, 1905

RECOMMENDED READING AND VIEWING

Ackerman, Diane. *Deep Play*. New York: Random House, 1999.

Apted, Michael, director. *Inspirations* (film). Home Vision Entertainment, 1997.

Arrien, Angeles. *The Nine Muses*. Santa Barbara: J. P. Tarcher & Co. 2000.

Bachelard, Gaston. *Fragments of a Poetics of Fire*. Dallas: The Dallas Institute, 1999.

————. *The Poetics of Reverie*. Boston: Beacon Press, 1960.

Bacon, John U. *Cirque du Soleil: The Spark*. New York: Doubleday, 2006.

Bayles, David & Ted Orland. *Art & Fear: Observations on the Perils (and Rewards) of Artmaking*. Santa Cruz: The Image Continuum, 1993.

Becker, Ernest. *The Denial of Death*. New York: The Free Press, 1973.

Bloom, Harold. *Genius*. New York: Warner Books, 2002.

Bolles, Richard Nelson. *What Color is Your Parachute 2007: A Practical Manual for Job-Hunters and Career-Changers*. Berkeley: Ten Speed Press, 2007.

Bradbury, Ray. *Fahrenheit 451*. New York: Ballantine Books, 1953.

————. *Zen in the Art of Writing: Essays on Creativity*. Santa Barbara: Capra Press, 1990.

Brande, Dorothea. *Becoming a Writer*. New York: Harcourt, Brace, and Company, 1934.

Bronowski, Jacob. *The Visionary Eye*. Cambridge: The MIT Press, 1981.

Brown, John. ed. *In the Chair: Interviews with Poets from the North of Ireland*. Dublin: Salmon Publishing, 2002.

Campbell, Joseph. *The Hero with a Thousand Faces*. Bollingen Series XVII. Princeton, N. J.: Princeton University Press, 1949.

———. *The Inner Reaches of Outer Space: Myth as Metaphor and as Religion*. New York: Alfred Van der Marck, 1986.

———. *Pathways to Bliss*. Novato: New World Library, 2004.

Cather, Willa. *Willa Cather on Writing*. New York: Alfred A. Knopf, Inc., 1920.

Cobb, Ty, with Al Stump. *My Life in Baseball*. New York: Doubleday and Company, Inc., 1961.

Cocteau, Jean. *The Art of Cinema: A Collection of Cocteau's Writings on Film*. Translated by Robin Buss. London & New York: Marion Boyars, 2001.

Coppola, Eleanor. *Notes*. New York: Simon & Schuster, 1982.

Cousineau, Phil. *Once and Future Myths*. Berkeley: Conari Press, 2001.

———. *The Olympic Odyssey*. Chicago: Quest Books, 2004.

———. *The Book of Roads: Travel Stories*. San Francisco: Sisyphus Press, 2000.

———. Ed. *The Hero's Journey: Joseph Campbell on His Life and Work*. San Francisco: Harper & Row, 1990.

Csikszentmihallyi, Mihaly. *Creativity*. New York: Harper Collins, 1996.

———. *Flow*. New York: Harper Collins, 1999.

da Vinci, Leonardo. Translated by J. G. Nichols. *Prophecies*. London: Hesperus Press Ltd., 2002.

Dear, John. *The Sound of Listening: A Retreat Journal from Thomas Merton's Hermitage*. Eugene: Wipf & Stock, Publishers, 1999.

Dillard, Annie. *The Writing Life*. New York: Harper Collins, 1989.

Dewey, John. *Art as Experience*. New York: The Berkeley Publishing Group, 1980.

Doctorow, E. L. *Creationists: Selected Essays, 1993–2006*.
New York: Random House Publishing Group, 2007.

Dov, Laila. *Laila Dov*. (Video) Group Five Films, San Francisco,
CA, 2006.

Dunway, Philip and Mel Evans. Editors. *A Treasury of the World's
Great Diaries*. New York: Doubleday and Company, Inc., 1957.

Eliot, T. S. *Four Quartets*. New York: Harcourt Brace, 1971.

Emerson, Ralph Waldo. *The Essential Writings of Ralph Waldo
Emerson*. New York, Modern Library, 1940.

Feibleman, Peter. *Lilly: Reminiscences of Lillian Hellman*. New York:
Avon Books, 1986.

Fritz, Robert. *Creativity*. New York: Fawcett Columbine, 1991.

Goodall, Jane. *In the Shadow of Man*. New York: Dell Publishing
Co., Inc., 1971.

Grudin, Robert. *The Grace of Great Things*. New York: Ticknor
& Fields, 1990.

———. *Time and the Art of Living*. New York: Ticknor & Fields, 1982.

Henri, Robert. *The Art Spirit*. New York: J. B. Lippincott Company,
1923.

Highwater, Jamake. *The Primal Mind: Vision and Reality in Indian
America*. New York: Harper & Row, 1981.

Hirsch, Edward. *The Demon and the Angel: A Search into the
Origins of Inspiration*. New York: Harcourt Press, 2002.

Johnson, Paul. *The Creators*. New York: Harper Collins, 2006.

Johnson, Robert A. *Ecstasy: Understanding the Psychology of Joy*.
San Francisco: Harper & Row Publishers, 1987.

Larsen, Stephen and Robin. *Fire in the Mind: The Life of Joseph
Campbell*. New York: Doubleday, 1991.

Intrator, Sam M. and Megan Scribner, ed. *Teaching with Fire:
Poetry that Sustains the Courage to Teach*. San Francisco:
Josey-Bass, 2000.

Leland, John. *Hip: The History*. New York: Harper Collins, 2004.

Lunson, Lian, director. *Leonard Cohen: I'm Your Man*. Lionsgate, 2005.

Lynch, David. *Catching the Big Fish*. Santa Barbara: Jeremy P. Tarcher. 2007.

Malick, Terrence, director and screenwriter. *The Thin Red Line* (film). Twentieth-Century Fox, 1998.

Mamet, David. *Three Uses of the Knife: On the Nature and Purpose of Drama*. New York: Vintage Books, 2000.

Marcy, Randolph B. *The Prairie Traveler: The 1859 Handbook for Westbound Pioneers*. Mineola, NY: Dover Publications, Inc., 2006.

May, Rollo. *The Courage to Create*. New York: W. W. Norton, 1975.

————. *My Quest for Beauty*. San Francisco: Saybrook Press, 1985.

Michalko, Michael. *Cracking Creativity: The Secrets of Creative Genius*. Berkeley, CA.: Ten Speed Press, 2001.

Morris, R. B. *The Last Fire*. Knoxville: Iris Books, 2007.

Mozart, Wolfgang Amadeus. *Letters of Wolfgang Amadeus Mozart*. Selected and edited by Hans Mernan. New York: Dover Publications, Inc., 1972.

Naber, John. Compiled by. *Awaken the Olympian Within: Stories from America's Greatest Olympic Motivators*. Torrance, CA: Griffin Publishing Group, 1999.

Nachmanovich, Stephen. *Free Play: Improvisation in Life and Art*. New York: Jeremy P. Tarcher and Penquin Putnam, 1990.

Nicosia, Gerald. *Memory Babe: A Life of Jack Kerouac*. New York: Grove Press, 2002.

Oates, Joyce Carol. *The Faith of a Writer: Life, Craft, Art*. Boston: Ecco Press, 2003.

Oeur, U Sam. *Sacred Vows*. Minneapolis: Coffee House Press, 1996.

Olivier, Lawrence. *Confessions of an Actor.* New York: Simon & Schuster, 1982.

O'Neill, Eugene. *Long Day's Journey into Night.* New Haven: Yale University Press, 1955.

Orwell, George. *Why I Write.* New York: Penquin Books, 2004.

Pouillon, Fernand. *The Stones of the Abbey.* Translated by Edward Gillot. New York: Haracourt, Brace & World, Inc., 1964.

Read, Herbert. *The Meaning of Art.* London: Pittman Publishing Company, 1951.

Rilke, Rainer Marie. *Letters to a Young Poet.* New York: W. W. Norton & Company, 2002.

Robinson, Todd, director. *Armagosa.* [The Life of Marta Becket] (video) Triple Play Pictures, 1999.

Rugoff, Ralph. *The Eye of the Needle: The Unique World of Micro-miniatures of Hagop Sandaldjian.* West Covina, CA.: The Society for the Diffusion of Useful Information Press, 1996.

Sarton, May. *Journal of a Solitude.* New York: W. W. Norton & Company, 1973.

Solnit, Rebecca. *A Field Guide to Getting Lost.* New York: Penquin Books, 2005.

Snyder, Gary. *The Real Work.* New York: New Directions Books, 1980.

Speerstra, Karen. *Divine Sparks: Collected Wisdom of the Heart.* Sandpoint, ID.: Morning Light Press: 2005.

Stafford, William. *The Answers Are Inside the Mountains: Meditations on the Writing Life.* Ed. By Paul Merchant and Vincent Wixon. Ann Arbor: University of Michigan Press, 2003.

Tarnas, Richard. *Prometheus: The Awakener.* Woodstock, CT.: Spring Publications, 1995.

Tharp, Twyla. *The Creative Habit.* New York: Simon & Schuster, 2007.

Tolstoy, Leo. *Confessions.* Shambhala Press, 1996.

Tucker, Michael. *Dreaming with Open Eyes*. New York: Harper Collins, 1992.

van Gogh, Vincent. *Dear Theo: The Autobiography of Vincent Van Gogh*. Ed. Irving Stone with Jean Stone. New York: Doubleday & Co., Inc. 1937.

Ueland, Brenda. *If You Want to Write*. Second Edition. Saint Paul, MN.: Graywolf Press, 1987.

Ventura, Michael. "The Talent of the Room," *L.A. Weekly,* May 21–May 27, 1993.

Vollard, Ambroise. *Renoir: An Intimate Record*. New York: Alfred Knopf, Inc. 1925.

Weschler, Lawrence. *Mr. Wilson's Cabinet of Wonder: Pronged Ants, Horned Humans, Mice on Toast, and Other Marvels of Jurassic Technology*. New York: Vintage Books, 1995.

Yates, Francis. *The Art of Memory*. Chicago: The University of Chicago Press, 1966.

Yu, Jessica, director and writer. *In the Realms of the Unreal*. [The Life of Henry Darger] (video) Cherry Sky Films, 2004.

PERMISSIONS

Grateful acknowledgment is made to the following for permission to reproduce images in the text:

To Gregg Chadwick for the use of the cover illustration, *Fire Dream, The Liquid Hour,* and *Balance;* to Dave Albers for *Rav* (Prometheus), copyright © Dave Alber; to Laila Carlson for *Fire Within,* copyright © Laila Carlson; to Jack Cousineau for his photograph *Silhouettes,* copyright © Jack Cousineau; to Pepin Press B.V. / Agile Rabbit Editions for use of *The Nine Muses, Prometheus and the Torch,* and *La rêve de Jacob;* to Maggie Oman Shannon for permission to use *Box Noetica;* to Chuck Davis for permission to use the photograph of *Rockfish;* to the Sandaljian Family & the Museum of Jurassic Technology for the photograph of Hagob Sandaljian, and for the photograph of his sculpture entitled *Baseball,* Museum of Jurassic Technology, 9341 Venice, L.A., CA 90034, info@mjt.org; to Harvard University Press for permission to use "To Make a Prairie" by Emily Dickinson, from *The Poems of Emily Dickinson,* edited by R. W. Franklin, 1999; to Jean Erdman Campbell, for permission to use the photograph of her by Harold Swann; to Larry Coleman for permission to use the photograph of *Homage to Nancy Oliveri,* copyright © Larry Coleman, 2007; to Stuart Vail Balcomb, for *Lady Sings the Blues* and *Focus;* to Paula Sartorius, for use of her photograph *Brian Wilson and Friends;* to Michael Ferreboeuf, for the photograph of his shadow box, *Writer's Block;* to Dr. Roberto Takaoka, for *Healing Art;* to Joanne Warfield, for the photograph *Faded Angel,* the Polaroid Wet Negative Transfer, *Persephone Rising;* to Gerald Nicosia for the photograph of Gerald Nicosia and Jan Kerouac; to Barb White, the Museum of Glass, Seattle, WA, and Betty Rosen for permission to use *Ahoy! Blow the Glass!;* to Karly Stribling, for permission to use the photograph of *Steel Guitar;* to Abigail Doggett Bordeaux for permission to use the photograph of her *Seven Pilgrimage Chapels;* and to Leigh Havle-Ferguson, for permission to use a photograph of her painting, *Reconciliation.*

All photographs not credited above were provided courtesy of the author.

ABOUT THE AUTHOR

Photo courtesy of Rich Reynolds.

Phil Cousineau is a Fellow of the Campbell Foundation and has appeared in *Newsweek* and on CNN, FOX, BBC, NPR, CBS, and other media outlets. He is heard as an expert on mythology on the DVD's of *Constantine, Superman, Double Indemnity, The Natural, Charles Schultz & Peanuts,* and *The Mythology of Heroes and Villains.* He lectures at Esalen, Omega, and Jung centers, and appears in 20–30 cities a year, including San Francisco, Syracuse, Knoxville, Los Angeles, Chicago, Cleveland, and Seattle. He will be hosting *Global Spirit,* a new thirteen-part television series on LINK-TV, in 2008. Visit him online at *www.philcousineau.com.*

TO OUR READERS

Conari Press, an imprint of Red Wheel/Weiser, publishes books on topics ranging from spirituality, personal growth, and relationships to women's issues, parenting, and social issues. Our mission is to publish quality books that will make a difference in people's lives—how we feel about ourselves and how we relate to one another. We value integrity, compassion, and receptivity, both in the books we publish and in the way we do business.

Our readers are our most important resource, and we value your input, suggestions, and ideas about what you would like to see published. Please feel free to contact us, to request our latest book catalog, or to be added to our mailing list.

Conari Press
An imprint of Red Wheel/Weiser, LLC
500 Third Street, Suite 230
San Francisco, CA 94107
www.redwheelweiser.com